T0302672

on track ...
Camel

every album, every song

Hamish Kuzminski

sonicbondpublishing.com

Sonicbond Publishing Limited
www.sonicbondpublishing.co.uk
Email: info@sonicbondpublishing.co.uk

First Published in the United Kingdom 2021
First Published in the United States 2021

British Library Cataloguing in Publication Data:
A Catalogue record for this book is available from the British Library

Copyright Hamish Kuzminski 2021

ISBN 978-1-78952-040-8

Typeset in ITC Garamond & ITC Avant Garde
Printed and bound in England

Graphic design and typesetting: Full Moon Media

Cover photograph: Bert Treep

on track ...
Camel

every album, every song

Hamish Kuzminski

sonicbondpublishing.com

CAMEL

1975 was the year that firmly established Camel as one of the country's brightest and most original bands. Their brilliant 'Snow Goose' album which remained in the charts for over 3 months put them in a World class category. This was further endorsed when they were voted "Brightest Hope" in the Melody Maker readers poll and on October 17th they performed in front of 6,000 people at London's Royal Albert Hall accompanied by the London Symphony Orchestra with conductor David Bedford.

On March 26th Camel release their fourth album 'Moon Madness' to coincide with a major concert tour of Britain.

Camel's present status in the Rock World has not been achieved overnight. Formed in 1972 by drummer Andy Ward, guitarist Andy Latimer and bassist Doug Ferguson, Camel were later joined by Peter Barden on keyboards, prior to the release of their first album, 'Camel'. Although musically perfect, that album was plagued with technical difficulties and it wasn't until the release of 'Mirage' that they started to receive the critical acclaim they deserved, with the album featuring in the US charts for 3 months.

Then came 'Snow Goose' a highly ambitious concept album inspired by Paul Gallico's famous short story. The project was from the start a risk, that took a year from conception to completion. However, any fears of the albums possible failure were allayed when the album went straight into the charts at No.19 where it remained for four months, becoming a top ten album and being voted 7th in the Top Albums by Melody Maker' readers.

Although 'Moon Madness' is not a concept album it is as ambitious as its predecessor and for the band it is an even greater achievement and by far their best album. It took less time to record than the 'Goose' which was partially due to Camel being responsible, for the first time, for the production. Andy Latimer explained why they decided to be involved with producing. "After three albums, it seemed natural to do everything ourselves, we're very pleased with it. We received a lot of help from Rhett Davies, our engineer, who co-produced it. There are seven tracks on the album, three of which are

Decca Promotion Department,
18 Great Marlborough Street, London W1V 2DL 01-734 9286

Maximising the capital from the success of *The Snow Goose*, Decca's press release reveals *Moonmadness* to the world in 1976. (*Private collection of Shane Carlson*)

Acknowledgements

My personal journey with Camel has lasted 45 years, and I hope that through the following pages, I am able to adequately impart to readers my abiding love of the band and its music; this is no 'Fanboi' book, though: at all times I have attempted to be objective and call it how it is.

Firstly, my unbounded thanks to Andy Latimer and Colin Bass who answered my questions graciously and humorously: Andy and Colin's vital input plugged gaps in the narrative, especially for the early days. Next, Ant Phillips spent considerable time with me filling in the cracks in my knowledge for the complicated times surrounding the *Single Factor* sessions: cheers, old boy! A special mention has to go to my sounding board and 'fixer', Shane Carlson, who is a fount of knowledge and owns what certainly has to be the most extensive collection of Camel memorabilia on the planet.

This book would, of course, not have been possible without the extraordinary patience and chivvying along of my publisher and editor, Stephen Lambe: you're a brick, mate, and one of the true unsung heroes of the progressive rock world. Also, I need to make special mention of my editor at *Progression* magazine, John Collinge, who believed in my abilities and gave me my opportunity in rock journalism: get well soon.

This leads me on to thank the many musicians I've had the pleasure to meet and occasionally inspire, particularly Steve Rothery for agreeing to write the Foreword, the talented Mr John Young of Lifesigns, the whole Pendragon gang, all of the splendid chaps and chapesses at IO-Earth, the inimitable and ridiculously under-rated Franck Carducci, Michael Sadler of Saga and Ollie Rusing of Karibow.

A special 'Ta, Buddy' is due to Pete Byrchmore of The Membranes – my oldest friend and 'technical consultant' who explained some of Andy Latimer's guitar tricks in language I was able to understand. Thanks as well to my family and friends whose incessant 'How's the book going?'-s gave me impetus throughout the process, and especially during the tougher sections. And of course, I couldn't have written this without the support, tolerance and belief of my wife, Damaris, as she has suffered through eighteen months of the same fifteen albums on constant rotation: she's not a fan, yet, but I think I'm getting there. Maybe.

WHEN THE CAMEL LIES DOWN WITH THE GOOSE

There are concept albums and concept albums, says ANGUS MACKINNON sagely. But if you want to do yourself a favour, hear CAMEL'S 'Snow Goose' right away . . .

IT'S ALWAYS reassuring to see a band take a few risks, and have them pay off with handsome dividends — like Peter Bardens' Camel and their recently-released 'Snow Goose' album.

Now there are concept albums and concept albums, some impossibly pretentious (yes, you know who I mean) and some, in their own quiet, unassuming way, rather successful. 'Snow Goose' falls happily into the latter category.

Maybe it's all to do with how you approach the thing — if you appreciate that you're probably not capable of producing the musical equivalent of 'War and Peace', then that's fine. But do what you can do and make sure you do it well. Which is how Camel seem to have dealt with their adaptation of Gallico's short story . . . honestly, painstakingly and with a minimum of fuss. But over to guitarist Andy Latimer for details.

"We wanted to do an album based on a story, and rather than write one ourselves — we did contemplate that at one stage — we decided to base it on a book. A lot of different books got put forward at the time. There was 'Siddartha', '1984', things like that. But as Peter and I were writing the music, obviously we had the most say.

Possibilities

"I got a very strong feeling from 'Snow Goose'. I could definitely see the musical possibilities. We all read it and enjoyed it, and so decided that was the one to do.

"We did, I think, go best some things more thoroughly than the book did, like 'Rhayader Goes To Town'. We were originally going to depart from it, and do other things, like elaborating on how the power got lost, but decided not to, just to stick quite rigidly to the book.

Devon

"We went down to Devon — incidentally I think it was written down there — and shut ourselves away, just writing. It was a fairly lengthy process, taking us about two weeks to write the music, but we were pleased with what we'd got. Peter and I worked things out between us, making sure everything related to the characters as we saw them. There're several themes in the album, which people will probably notice after a bit. The 'Snow Goose' melody appears three or four times in a minor form.

"There are definite places that Peter wrote, and definite ones that I wrote, and then some we wrote together. If Peter brought in a piece and I didn't see anything in it, I'd say so, and vice versa. We went through it all roughly as the same order as it appears on the album, although the intro took us a bit of time to pull together."

"Was it easy to record?"

"Well, we rehearsed for another two weeks in Devon, then went virtually straight into the studio. It was very different from 'Mirage'; there we'd been doing things for six months on the road before getting them down. We started recording before we went to the States, and had done about a third of it by the time we left, backing tracks and so on. It took around two months in all."

"Was it a conscious decision not to include any lyrics?"

"We felt we couldn't say any more than Gallico. There was some talk of a narrative but that sort of thing really does just hand in. After you've heard it once, that's it. We were going to do a brief synopsis for the sleeve insert, but decided to do without one. Actually Gallico knows about it, although we haven't met him. Maybe he'd welcome a bit or some of it. I don't know."

Smiles all round.

And how about David Bedford's contribution?

"Andy Ward (Camel's drummer) suggested him. We wanted an arranger as we were planning to orchestrate the album, and we wanted someone whose approach was slightly sort of sideways. We didn't want yer Mantovani string section, which it could have been. So we phoned him and asked if he'd like to do it. He listened to the tapes, which we left with him whilst we were in America, telling him which bits we wanted orchestrated.

Feeling

"He was very good, because he captured the feel of it. We're very pleased with what he's done. He's very quiet, very nice to work with. We did the orchestration in Decca's studios. It was very quick. The strings didn't have any difficulties, but the brass had quite a job — some of the trumpet lines are fairly hard, for session players anyway.

"There was one trombonist who made me laugh. He had this newspaper, which he was reading as everything went on around him in full flight. Then, about five bars before he was due to come in, he put it down, picked up his trombone, and away he went. Complete disinterest! But most of them were great. It's exciting to listen to your own piece being orchestrated, really good for the ego.

"The Roundhouse concert with the orchestra didn't come off, mainly due to the lack of stage space there, and also because they'd wanted to arrange both 'Lady Fantasy' and 'White Rider' for orchestra — there just wasn't time to do it. However it's possible that Camel may tour to the States at some stage with an orchestra, depending on finances, and they hope to do a date with Bedford over here in the summer.

In fact, Camel have their eye very much on America at present. Their first tour there last year was particularly auspicious. Chrysalis, their Stateside label, were right behind them, helping to get a string of dates with Wishbone Ash, and the response in New York, LA and Chicago was really favourable. The next trip will be slightly slimmer though, as they found these months' touring somewhat arduous.

But 'Snow Goose' is forty minutes of new music — isn't that asking a lot from an audience?

Demanding

"Yes, it is, but it'll be easier when people become more familiar with the material. It's a big jump for the band too, not just adding a new number to the set each night or something like that. It's also quite demanding to play, but very rewarding, whilst it's still fresh. I'm doing some stuff for the next album already; it'll be brief, with more vocals again, probably not a concept thing. I'm still recovering from the one we did in France with Soft Machine. Alan Holdsworth was absolutely fantastic. I just used to stand in the wings every night, and man, a shame he's left.

"The 'Snow Goose' was a natural progression for us, and the next one'll be completely different."

If Manchester, where 'Snow Goose' sold 550 copies the day after Camel played there, is anything to go by, we might see the album in the charts. About time too! Camel are long overdue for some kind of wider recognition. In fact 'Snow Goose' puts work by quite a few so-called first division bands to shame.

Do yourself a favour and hear it, right away.

on track ...
Camel

Contents

On what better steed to commence our journey across the shifting sands of
progressive rock than the ship of the desert itself ...
Bill Bailey
(Bill Bailey's *Prog Rock Top 10*, Channel 4, 2001)

Above: 'The ship of the desert', indeed. Cover of the Japanese
program for the *Breathless* tour in 1978. (*Private collection of
Shane Carlson*)

Foreword By Steve Rothery

It was 1975 and I was fifteen years old, growing up in Whitby, a small fishing town on the Yorkshire coast. I'd started playing the guitar while still at school and had recently discovered progressive rock, thanks mainly to Alan Freeman's Saturday afternoon rock radio show and had made the decision, much to my school career adviser's amusement, that I was going to become a professional musician after I left school the following year.

The three main bands that excited me at the time (primarily because of the guitar playing) were Pink Floyd, Genesis and Camel. Of the three, Camel were by far the strongest influence. Andy Latimer's lyrical and melodic approach was a huge inspiration as I struggled first of all to learn the instrument, then to try to develop as a player and writer. I remember listening to the *Mirage* and *Snow Goose* albums constantly and buying the *Moonmadness* album when it came out and really enjoying it.

At the end of 1978, my first band split after two of them left to go to university, so I found myself, at the age of nineteen, at a very loose end. I came across an advert in a music paper for a band called Silmarillion who were looking for a guitarist with a Genesis/Camel style, very different from the punk/ new wave era at the time. I drove the 250 miles from Whitby to a little cottage in Hertfordshire; auditioned and got the job!

We bonded over our love of Camel, Genesis and Rush and my style really started to develop (very heavily influenced, it has to be said, by Andy's playing).

After our original drummer, Mick Pointer, left in 1983 at the end of the tour for our first album, *Script for a Jester's Tear*, we tried out a selection of drummers in what became an almost *Spinal Tap*-like experience. Andy Ward was collecting some of his drum equipment at the Nomis rehearsal studio in London one day and when he heard we were auditioning drummers, he decided to try out. His amazing groove and tasteful playing meant he was offered the job on the spot. He played with us for several months, including our only *Old Grey Whistle Test* TV appearance and our only billing at the Glastonbury Festival, but we parted ways during a stressful US tour.

I've had the pleasure of meeting Andy Latimer a few times over the years and had the honour of presenting him with a Lifetime Achievement Award at the 2014 Progressive Music awards. Camel will always hold a special place in my heart and Andy should be very proud of his incredible musical legacy and vision.

Steve

Prologue

It's July 2018 high on the Loreley Rock, the home of ancient myths and legends overlooking the Rhine in central Germany, and the sunset reflecting off the river, colouring the clouds in deep shades of orange, red and blue at the end of a blistering hot day is spectacular. You can viscerally feel the anticipation in the crowd – awe, even – at what everyone hopes is about to happen. But there's a degree of anxiety as well: the band leader had to cut short the tour earlier in the year due to a sudden bout of pneumonia, not the first life-threatening illness he has experienced in recent years: would he be up to it? What about the rest of the band, with a relatively new keyboard player on board: would they be able to rise to the occasion and own the amphitheatre, or might they keep their heads down, go through the motions and play it safe? Anticipation; hope.

Then the marching beat of 'Aristillus' strikes up and the obligatory dry ice fills the stage; the capacity crowd roars as the two-minute introduction to *Moonmadness* – the 1976 classic being played tonight in its entirety – comes to an end: 'Aristillus, Autolycus, Aristillus, Autolycus, Aristillus, Autolycus' ... then the strains of 'Song Within a Song' begin, and the spotlight focuses as a man, looking a little frail, seated and with legs crossed, brings a flute to his mouth. It's a moment of utter, unbounded, jaw-dropping beauty in a festival setting like no other.

Half an hour-or-so later, the audience erupts in a standing ovation as the Apollo XI radio feed sample that closes 'Lunar Sea', and thus the live rendition of the complete album, crackles to a close. We needn't have worried: Camel, led by Andy Latimer, were triumphant. We've watched and listened to a band who, both instrumentally and performance-wise, are at their peak. It is incredible given many years of uncertainty that they were note and meter perfect, tighter than a drum and enjoying every second. Incredibly *Moonmadness* sounded even fresher and uplifting than when first released. This, people, is the real thing and we have witnessed something that only a decade previously was considered gone forever. Camel continue to play for another 90-odd minutes, with a setlist that spans a broad spectrum of the back catalogue, putting some amazing new twists on old favourites. The band was back, and some.

Introduction

At first glance, you might not think that Mikael Åkerfeldt of Swedish prog-metalers Opeth and Rick 'Never Gonna Give You Up' Astley – yes, he of the *Rickroll* meme – would have much in common musically, but you'd be dead wrong: they do. The intersection of this particular Venn diagram is Camel. Interviewed by *Guitar World*, Åkerfeld named *Moonmadness* as the 'album that changed my life', and Astley says the visit to his first gig – a 1975 performance of *The Snow Goose* in Manchester – 'blew my mind'. So there you go: Stock, Aitken & Waterman meet Nordic black metal via a prog band from Guildford. Funny old world.

Formed in 1971, Camel, although not part of the Canterbury Scene, built their unique, quintessentially English sound clearly influenced by Caravan, Hatfield and the North, Soft Machine and others in the genre. Their mixture of humour and profundity is a hallmark. However, and there's a clue in the name, as their music seamlessly integrates Middle Eastern and North African themes, forms, scales and rhythms, as well as jazz, blues, fusion, folk and classical elements. This created an exciting and exotic new strand to the ballooning world of progressive rock in the early 1970s.

There was, of course, a pre-history ahead of the band coalescing in 1971, and this journey commenced in 1964 when Andrew Latimer (lead guitar and vocals), together with his brother Ian (bass and vocals), and friends Alan Butcher (drums) and Richard Over (rhythm guitar) formed The Phantom Four. Over didn't stay long, and was replaced by Graham Cooper, also playing rhythm, thus maintaining the original shape of the band. This personnel change also precipitated a name change, and Strange Brew were born. Interestingly the classic Cream song, 'Strange Brew', wasn't released until 1967, so we're left wondering who influenced whom, or if this was just a coincidence fuelled by an abundance of the *strange brews* that were circulating the South East of England in those early 'Summer of Love' days.

Although the band performed mainly cover versions, there were some self-penned numbers that sadly have been lost to the proverbial mists of time. Nevertheless, according to Camel's potted history on the Camel Productions web site, through regular gigging, they achieved a staunch local following that would be the nucleus of the band's future success.

In 1968, with Ian Latimer and Cooper both hearing the impending chime of wedding bells (as well as, one imagines, the ping of timeclocks), the remaining Latimer plus Butcher advertised in the local newspaper, the *Surrey Advertiser*, for a new bass player. Enter Doug Ferguson, hired on the basis of having some (then) state-of-the-art gear and a 'fat' bass sound: the nucleus of the classic line-up was formed.

Becoming a three-piece precipitated two changes: first, the name, perhaps because of confusion with the now hit Cream record, was shortened to The Brew, and second the decision to focus on Blues – albeit with a funky twist – as their musical direction. It wasn't long before Butcher left, unwilling to take the risk of being a full-time musician, and the search was on for a new occupant of the drum stool. Providentially, through his recent musical peregrinations, Ferguson knew someone who might fit the bill, and so on 15 January 1969, Andy Ward – then a mere whippersnapper at sixteen years old, and after a shoo-in of an audition – joined the band. On *Curriculum Vitae* (henceforth, '*CV*'), Latimer recalls:

> He was brilliant, hitting everything in sight – everything was shaking – double kick drums – it was fantastic!

Ward later claimed he was doing an impression of Ginger Baker, but whatever he did or didn't do at the audition, it clearly worked and he was in. Three-quarters of the classic line up was now in place.

With Ward on board, Ferguson cemented his contribution to the band not only through his incredible groove on the bass but also by acting as de-facto A&R, manager and fiscal enforcer with a talent for extracting financial dues out of some of the more reluctant and 'short-armed, deep-pocketed' promoters of the day. Latimer has often commented on the importance of Ferguson's military background in this respect.

On the back of this raised profile, The Brew were gigging regularly and in 1970 recorded their first demo, a cover of Eric Clapton's 'Crossroads'. This demo piqued the interest of Dick James' DJM Records, who had just released Elton John's eponymous first album: things were looking up. However, this opportunity turned out to be a mixed blessing when it emerged that James wanted the band to act merely as a backing group for one of his existing roster, Philip Goodhand-Tait. Ferguson, on *CV*, said of the opportunity:

> We didn't think this would be a job for life, just a stepping stone; but a very important one.

Nevertheless, the association did bear fruit in the form of an album titled *I Think I'll Write a Song*, released in 1971. Without question, the highlight of the record – an LP rip of which is easily found on the internet, the physical LP less so – is Latimer's guitar work, even at this early stage, showcasing his technical, melodic and stylistic talents. Unfortunately, the record wasn't a success, with one critic, rather unkindly and no doubt as a sideways dig at DJM, dubbing Goodhand-Tait as a 'poor man's Elton John'. Despite this less-than-resounding vote of confidence, Goodhand-Tait went on to record a few more albums for DJM and then Chrysalis in the 70s but is probably best known as a live album producer, including concert offerings from artists as diverse as Magnum, Venom, Climax Blues Band and Kid Creole and the Coconuts.

For Latimer, Ferguson and Ward, however, one critical formative driver came out of the association: Goodhand-Tait was a piano player, and now they wanted keyboards as part of the band's mix. To that end, they placed an advert in *Melody Maker*.

Peter Bardens, some five years older than Latimer et al. and an established feature on the London scene, had an impressive resumé with credits alongside Van Morrison, Rod Stewart, Peter Green and Mick Fleetwood, the latter as the drummer in The Cheynes who recorded three singles for the Columbia label. As well as the group work, Bardens had a couple of solo LPs to his name – *The Answer* (1970) and *Peter Bardens* (1971), both on Transatlantic Records. On 20 September 1971, Bardens saw the ad and raised his hand. It was instant chemistry, and the classic line-up, although not yet named Camel, was born. On *CV* Bardens said of his first meeting:

I was especially impressed with how Andy Ward and Doug worked as a rhythm section. Every kick drum beat was worked out to the nth degree.

But the band were even more bowled over. Latimer elaborates, again on *CV*:

A friend of Andy Ward's had a Hammond in his basement, and so we set up and then Pete came in, looking all dishevelled, like he'd just woken up, looked like he'd slept in his clothes ... so we had a jam, and from the first note all of us had smiles and we just knew we had something.

At that time, Bardens was committed to a handful of gigs in Ireland, and so it was that almost indecently soon after coming together as a four-piece, the band were off across the Irish Sea, performing their first date together in Belfast as 'Peter Bardens' On...' on 8 October 1971. The setlist for the Irish gigs comprised a mix of Bardens' original compositions (including the epic 'Homage To The God of Light', later to appear on the remaster of Camel's first album in 2002 and also on the *Greasy Truckers* double album, recorded at Dingwalls in Camden, London, along with Henry Cow, Global Village Trucking Company and Gong, a few Brew numbers, and a handful of covers to round things off. 'We were so excited to be playing in Ireland, so soon after forming', says Latimer.

Now the band needed a name. No-one in the band admits to coming up with the name, alternatives for which were discussed ad nauseum and usually under the influence. On *CV*, Latimer said of the process:

After every rehearsal, we sat around for hours in pubs and it would always degenerate into stupidness ... who could come up with the silliest name.

The only name which any member of the band can recall, apart from what we know is coming next, was Battleship. This was a Ferguson suggestion that thankfully was rejected in short order. Although Latimer reckons that it was Ward that should claim credit for Camel, Ward said it was Bardens, who also denies responsibility. Only Ferguson – no doubt licking his wounds after the naval suggestion – seems to have escaped the long, gnarled finger of suspicion.

Ultimately, according to Ward on the *CV* DVD, and after the band slept on it, the die was cast because:

> They're [camels] funky animals, and the desert imagery appealed to us.

So, by November and mutual agreement, the four-piece became Camel. Choosing this as the name courted some small controversy in the early days as Peter Frampton also called his band 'Peter Frampton's Camel': arguments ensued, but soon after the Frampton ungulate plodded over a dune and into the sunset, leaving the boys as the sole claimants to the name.

The name also precipitated some questionable marketing tactics from the publicists, including one photo shoot incident which Latimer shared with Cerys Matthews on *BBC Radio 6* in 2013:

> Germany was one of the funniest ... because somebody had set up this shoot where we were pouring champagne over a poor young camel to christen it, and after, it was supposed to be us getting on to a camel. Well, these camels were not into it at all and one of the camels did 'something' on the ground. Pete got on that camel's back, promptly got thrown off, into the 'droppings', but nobody got a shot of it. Of course, we were in hysterics.

Waltham Forest Technical College, situated just beyond London's East End, wasn't exactly The Roundhouse or Marquee in terms of venue status, but in early 1970s UK, the so-called 'college circuit' was a thriving and lucrative scene for established as well as new bands: talking to *Melody Maker* in 1973, Bardens said:

> I think the college circuit plays a very important part in any new band's future. They are one of those rare places where small bands get the chance to play, and what's more, they're always good payers.

And so it was on 4 December 1971 that the freshly-monikered Camel played their first gig, supporting Wishbone Ash just as that band was about to hit the big time with *Argus* the following year. Moving into 1972, Camel gigged regularly, mainly around London and the South East of England. As a result of this hard work and favourable reviews in the music press, the band gained a steadily growing following.

In parallel to the live performances, Latimer, Ferguson and Ward – *sans* Bardens, because the producer 'didn't like organs' – and continuing the format of the Goodhand-Tait work, made some additional cash by doing session work for producer Richard Ferris at EMI. Such was the already solid camaraderie between the four that the income from these sessions was shared with Bardens. It was through this collaboration with EMI that the band came into the orbit of leading and high-profile producer Mickie Most, TV personality, and owner of the RAK Records and its music publishing businesses. Immediately seeing Latimer's potential as a songwriter, Most signed him alone to the publishing company, but intriguingly, neither Latimer nor the band to the record label.

However, Most's (pardon me) most important contribution to the development of Camel was his introduction to booker Geoff Jukes who had recently struck out on his own forming the Gemini Agency. Jukes was an immediate fan of the music and set out to raise their profile on the live circuit. The collaboration was an incredible success, with Camel during the spring and summer of 1972 getting on stage at premier venues including the aforementioned Marquee Club, the London School of Economics and the Fulham Greyhound, as well as Croydon's legendary Fairfield Halls and the Civic Hall in their hometown of Guildford.

By August, the boys had asked Jukes to be their manager and MCA Records came knocking. MCA, although a relative newcomer to the UK industry, already had Wishbone Ash, Osibisa, Stackridge and Budgie on their imprint, so there was clear momentum behind the label. Camel, though, were offered only a one LP deal, with an option on a second and third; in the long run, this turned out to be a blessing in disguise.

On 15 August 1972, Camel entered Morgan Studios in North London to put music to tape, kicking off a run of 15 studio albums that have entered the premier canon of British progressive rock. Of course, the story doesn't end here, so I will continue the history of the band in the introductions to each album.

Given the evolution of the band, by necessity, not all albums or tracks will receive equal attention – as with the output of most if not all artists, some numbers are forgettable, many are classics and a handful, masterpieces; this is reflected in my narrative. Also, I haven't gone into any significant depth regarding musical theory – time signatures, keys, song structure and so forth – unless this is vital to an enhanced appreciation of the song in question. I suspect most readers will prefer to know more about the *moods* than the *modes*. With *Snow Goose*, however, I feel it is worthwhile to delve deep into the composition.

All of the earlier albums are reviewed on the basis of the 2000s remasters, unless specified otherwise. These versions are, without exception, superior in sound quality to the originals, so although some readers may object to authenticity, this author's opinion is that this is the best way to appreciate this wonderful band's output. Additionally, these come with a treasure trove of extra, previously unavailable content, that unlike many special editions with bonus tracks, only add to the enjoyment. There's no dross or chaff here – it's all relevant, especially the live sessions. Don't expect any redundant 'acoustic third take with engineer audible and janitor coughing' type stuff.

At this point, I'd like to give a shout out to Mark Powell: as a freelancer contracted to Decca (for the 2002 re-issues) and then as founder of Esoteric

Records, the owner of the 2009 re-issue rights, Mark has curated the Camel catalogue with outstanding care and attention. I use 'curated' in the fullest sense, as he was responsible not only for the tape research but also for the production, sleeve notes and the running order of bonus content. In the case of *A Live Record*, the remaster is revelatory for those who own only the original 1978 version.

Before we get down to the nitty-gritty, as a preface, I'd like to quote Canadian writer Allister Thompson, author of the great *Make Your Own Taste* blog who, I feel, captures the essence of Camel in the following passage:

What distinguishes Camel's music is really Latimer's musical personality, at least since he's taken to running the band on his own. There's an important idea that such intellectual luminaries as Camus and Orwell have tried to present in their works, which is decency. By this, I mean the basic need that people have at their best to be good to each other, whether in times of duress or in their small daily interactions, thus providing meaning in a world that often seems depressingly meaningless. It may be weird to associate this concept with rock music, but it's true in this case. While Latimer's music is tuneful and well-composed and definitely of interest to discerning listeners, there's just a sense of quiet decency and compassion in his songs, his playing and his voice that makes this music for true grown-ups, not in the easy listening sense, but in that there is a lot of wisdom to be found here. A reassuring tranquillity and an interest in human betterment, I'd say. I'm not sure that makes any sense, but that's my feeling.

Cast Of Characters
Andrew Latimer (Born 1949)
Guitar, vocals, flute, keyboards, drum machine, penny whistle, pan pipes, koto, recorder. 1971-

If any one member of the band can lay claim to being the heart and soul of Camel, it is Andy Latimer. As the only remaining original member, he is still at the helm as Camel mark their 50th anniversary in 2021.

Born in Guildford, England, some 25 miles southwest of London, Latimer is cited by many rock guitarists as a key influence. Latimer's trademark melancholy, melodic, lyrical and emotional style is a, if not *the* critical element of the Camel sound, certainly for the later, post-Bardens records.

Latimer picked up a guitar at fourteen years old – grabbing his brother's acoustic and playing, of all things, 'Jingle Bells'. Immediately seeing the potential, his father sent him off for lessons. Early influences, unsurprisingly, were Hank Marvin of The Shadows, The Beatles and Merseybeat. His weapons of choice are a Gibson Les Paul and a red Fender Stratocaster, an instrument he would explicitly mention in verse on *Rajaz*.

With his guitar talents not in dispute, it shouldn't be overlooked that he is a songwriter/composer of incredible accomplishment, musically as well as in terms of his lyric writing: both early on in partnership with Peter Bardens, and later on alone, he manages to create 'mini symphonies' in rock form, packing melodic, key, tempo and mood changes galore into comparatively shorts songs without them ever seeming cluttered. On the larger-scale concept works, this quasi-classical approach to composition reaches its zenith with the use of leitmotifs, variations and reprises.

But it's not just the guitar at which Andy excels: apart from the six-string, he is best known as a flautist – another ingredient in the Camel cocktail that adds to their distinctiveness compared to some of the more bombastic contributors to the progressive music scene. Add to this his ability to play keyboards and recorder, and a penchant for the exotic through his use of the koto and Pan Pipes, Latimer is a multi-instrumentalist of the highest order: 'I'm the sort of musician that can play anything – not necessarily well, but I can get a tune out of it!', said Latimer to *Record Collector* magazine in 2013.

Touring *Stationary Traveller* in 1984 marked the end of Camel's first era. Feeling disillusioned with his country of birth and seeking new inspiration, Latimer and his partner Susan Hoover moved to the USA in 1988 and set up Camel Productions: I'll go into more detail about this period later on in the book. Latimer and Hoover spent eighteen years in California before returning to the UK in 2006, in the main due to a desire to be closer to friends and family.

In 2007, shocking news rocked the Camel community. Unbeknownst to all but his closest family and friends, Latimer had for some time suffered from a progressive blood disorder – polycythaemia vera – which had unexpectedly progressed to myelofibrosis, an aggressive form of blood cancer. In

November 2007, he underwent a successful bone marrow transplant at Bristol Royal Infirmary, ultimately recovering completely.

Although no longer in medical danger, it still took Latimer a few years before he considered a revival of the band. This came in 2013 when the Bass / Clement / LeBlanc line-up reconvened to re-record *Snow Goose*, touring once more later in the year.

Interviewed by *Hit-Channel.com* in 2013, Steven Wilson said, 'Andrew Latimer means very much to me' and official recognition from his industry peers came in 2014 when he was presented with the Lifetime Achievement Award at The Progressive Music Awards, joining a pantheon of individual Prog Award winners that includes Eddie Jobson, Carl Palmer, Rick Wakeman, Steve Howe and Tony Banks. In his endearing tongue-in-cheek fashion, he started his acceptance speech in a typically understated manner by saying, 'It's not bad, getting old'.

Latimer and Hoover now live in the beautiful county of Wiltshire, England, with Camel Productions – and Andy – still in rude health. Latimer's most recent – at time of writing – studio recording is as a guest on Ton Scherpenzeel's band Kayak's album, *Seventeen*. On the track 'Ripples On The Water', he plays a stunning acoustic accompaniment followed by one of his trademark melancholic solos: seek it out for a fresh fix of the man's genius.

Peter Bardens (1945-2002)
Keyboards, vocals. 1971-1978, 1982, 1984 (live, one show)
Born on 19 June 1945 in the shadow of the Second World War, Peter Bardens was brought up in the – at that time – edgy London district of Notting Hill, attending the local Byam Shaw art school where he studied Fine Art. He was the son of Dennis Bardens, a BBC editor and founder of the BBC television programme *Panorama* (the show which inspired the American television show *60 Minutes*). His father also wrote mystery novels and biographies, including, in 1965, one of Princess Margaret. Creative blood clearly flowed in the family.

Bardens' first band of any consequence was The Cheynes, formed in 1963 with a then-undiscovered Mick Fleetwood: the group's third and final single was titled 'Down And Out' with a B-side of 'Stop Running Around' co-produced and co-written by Bill Wyman, who also played bass on the number. Sadly, even with the Rolling Stones connection, the 45 failed to sell in sufficient volumes and The Cheynes split up.

Van Morrison already knew Bardens, as in 1964, as session keyboard player, he had recorded 'Baby Please Don't Go' alongside Jimmy Page on guitar, so was asked to join Morrison's touring band, Them. Incidentally, 'Baby Please Don't Go' was the first and only time that a founding Camel band member ever played on a UK Top Ten record.

After his time with the Irishman came Peter B's Looners, again with Fleetwood on drums, together with an unknown guitarist called Peter Green: Green wasn't to stay unknown for long.

Deeply influenced by Jimmy Smith, Booker T Jones and James Brown, Bardens was one of the first rock keyboard players to really embrace the Hammond B3 organ, becoming a virtuoso in the process. The Hammond was a critical element of the early Camel sound, with Andy Latimer saying on *CV*:

> With the Hammond, it was great for me as a guitarist as it didn't interfere with the sound spectrum at all.

In 1971, after releasing a couple of solo albums, Bardens joined Camel, where he, together with Andy Latimer, would form one of the greatest compositional partnerships of 70s progressive rock. Bardens left Camel in somewhat acrimonious circumstances near the end of the *Breathless* sessions in 1978, playing again with Van Morrison on the album *Wavelength* and the subsequent tour. Bardens' final studio contribution to Camel was on 'Sasquatch' from *The Single Factor* in 1982, then making a surprise one-off appearance with the band at the Hammersmith Odeon in 1984 (details in the Live Albums section later in this book). In 1985 Bardens emigrated to Malibu, California, where he released a number of well-received solo records and reunited with Mick Fleetwood, recording the 1988 album *Speed of Light* as well together writing soundtracks that capitalised on Bardens' talent for composing vivid and evocative soundscapes ... including a contribution to *Nightmare on Elm Street 2*.

In addition to his solo career, Bardens took a walk down memory lane with Andy Ward in 1994, when they collaborated in the imaginatively named Mirage, performing a few dates in Europe during that year, then gigging in the US, but without Ward.

Bardens continued to perform around southern California and completed his final LP, *The Art of Levitation*, in 2001. For Camel completists, though, the Holy Grail is his unreleased album *Black Elk*, tapes of which are rumoured to pop up now and again in the Camelsphere.

Bardens' valedictory gig – a benefit concert for his cancer treatment – was on 28 September 2001 at the intimate Canyon Club in Agoura Hills, not far from his home in Malibu. Joining him on stage were a selection of the great and good of the rock music world: John McVie, John Mayall, Joe Walsh, Sheila E, Ben Harper and, of course, Mick Fleetwood, with Whoopi Goldberg contributing a recorded introduction.

Bardens died of cancer in January 2002. Such was the respect in which Bardens was held, even the British broadsheets felt compelled to write lengthy obituaries. *The Independent* wrote of Bardens:

> The keyboard player's greatest influence on the British music scene took place in the Sixties, when he was a formative member of London's art school R&B scene and a figure of irrepressible spirit and energy ... Fired by the burgeoning blues movement in west London, Bardens recruited an apprentice drummer called Mick Fleetwood whom he had heard rehearsing in the garage of a house

three doors away from where he lived. With the intention of joining a group, Fleetwood had moved to London in 1964 to stay with his sister: 'There was a knock on the door. 'I've been hearing you play: would you like a gig?' He literally kickstarted me into the music business'.

Fleetwood later eulogised, also in *The Independent*:

> He [Bardens] never became a huge star, but he was always known as one of the better keyboard players in the world. He also was a great talent scout: he found two members of Fleetwood Mac and was my mentor. And he was an incredibly funny guy.

Rest in peace, Pete.

Doug Ferguson (Born 1947)

Bass, vocals, duffle coat. 1971-1976

Born in Carlisle, England, after leaving school Doug Ferguson had a short stint in the army, stationed in Aden in the Middle East (where, let's face it, he must have seen a camel or two) before embarking on a career as a bassist. His first band was Andy Ward's Misty Romance, and in an interview with the *Art Into Dust* blog in 2008, Ward remembers the first meeting clearly:

> He had short hair, a nice pink Fender jazz bass and most importantly, his own transport, so he was in. He'd just had time after leaving the army to try and make himself look hip by growing these long cheesy sideburns, I remember, but then that's Doug all over, bless 'im.

In 1968, Doug joined The Brew, which as we know evolved into Camel. Ferguson's contribution to the band was not solely as one half of the rhythm section. In the early days, he managed the band from within, and as time went on he became the peacemaker and 'glue' for Camel – soft skills that were to be sorely missed when he was unceremoniously sacked after *Moonmadness.*

Although he preferred playing with a pick, not finger plucking, footage from the *Old Grey Whistle Test* appearances in 1973 and 1975 clearly show he was quite capable of that style too.

After the initial hurt from his departure, Doug remained friends with the other members: it's great to see him jamming back in 2003 with Latimer and Ward on the *Curriculum Vitae* DVD.

Ferguson went on to be a successful property developer in the north of England, where he still lives and is now retired from business.

Andy Ward (Born 1952)

Drums, percussion, vocals, thunder sheet, hose and bucket of water. 1971-1981
Epsom, England-born Andy Ward was only sixteen when Doug Ferguson

suggested he join The Brew. After the shortest of auditions, he was in. His jazz-influenced style was a perfect counterpoint to the more blues-oriented concoctions that The Brew were fermenting at the time, thereby having a central influence on the direction the band would take once born as Camel.

Highly regarded in progressive rock and fusion circles, while with Camel, Andy was asked by Phil Collins to play a gig with Brand X: this turned out to be an inadvertent slapstick performance, and the story is told in full later in this book.

During the *Nude* tour, Ward's behaviour started to cause serious problems within the band: he was drinking heavily and having manic episodes. Soon after the tour, he attempted suicide: although all the signs had been there, none of his bandmates had realised he was suffering from bipolar disorder, putting his actions down to alcohol alone.

Once his rehabilitation was regarded as complete, Andy was soon back on the drum stool, but never again with Camel. First, in 1983 he joined Marillion, leading to his one and only appearance on *Top of the Pops* and a school-cap-and-shorts-wearing role in the video for 'Garden Party': although Mick Pointer was the drummer on *Script for a Jester's Tear*, he had been sacked in acrimonious circumstances at the end of the *'Script...'* tour and therefore wasn't around for the TV appearance and video shoot. Ward's tenure on the Marillion drum stool lasted less than a year: he had been recruited to the band due to his stature in Camel, but his personal problems resurfaced during Marillion's first US tour and he suffered a nervous breakdown midway through their travels.

This relapse led to a six-year absence from the music business, but Ward returned in fine form in 1990, joining ex-Camel bandmate Richard Sinclair's Going Going, which soon morphed into Caravan of Dreams. After this, in 1994, Ward briefly reunited with Peter Bardens in the short-lived Mirage before joining alt-rock-psychedelic stalwarts The Bevis Frond, a stint that spanned six years from 1996 to 2002.

Childhood friend Chris Morton has written a wonderful extended essay on his relationship with Ward, which is a fascinating read, and the URL can be found in the 'Other Reading' section at the end of this book.

In 2003, alongside Doug Ferguson, Ward joined up with Latimer for two weeks in California to film a segment for the *Curriculum Vitae* DVD. The idea was to distil a new batch of The Brew and record a blues album – according to Ward, something like twelve tracks were laid down in The Little Barn, but unfortunately, the album never came to pass, although Latimer still has the files. Nevertheless, the deep friendship and chemistry between the three are palpable.

Richard Sinclair (Born 1948)
Bass, vocals. 1977-1979

As a founder member of Caravan, Richard Sinclair can properly be regarded as one of the chief progenitors of the Canterbury Scene. As comfortable behind the mic as he is on the bass guitar, Sinclair's dulcet, almost choirboy-like tones added extra colour to Camel's vocal palette. Such was his impact on the band's sound that it's hard to realise that he was with the band for only three years and two studio albums – *Rain Dances* and *Breathless*.

With Caravan, his talents as a songwriter blossomed on *In The Land Of Grey And Pink*, where he penned the title track, tongue-in-cheek 'Golf Girl' and the anthemic 'Winter Wine'. Leaving the band in 1972, he formed another Canterbury Scene stalwart, Hatfield And The North. The 'North fizzled out in 1975 and disillusioned with the music business, he went into semi-retirement, filling his time as a jobbing carpenter and kitchen fitter, a profession he would sporadically return to over the coming years: a pair of his speaker cabinets would be a mighty catch for any self-respecting prog fan.

In 1991, Sinclair formed Caravan of Dreams, with Andy Ward and former Hatfield roadie Rick Biddulph on bass. Occasionally joined by cousin Dave and Kit Watkins, Camel alumni both, Caravan of Dreams came to an end in 1995. Hatfield and the North reformed in 2005 but disbanded the following year after the sad death of Pip Pyle.

David Sinclair (Born 1947)
Keyboards, vocals. 1978-1979
David, cousin of Richard, was brought into Camel together with Jan Schelhaas as one half of the brace of ex-Caravan keyboard players recruited as a result of Peter Bardens' sudden departure during the *Breathless* sessions. From a progressive music perspective, Sinclair, D's claim to fame is the writing of Caravan's 20-minute plus epic, 'Nine Feet Underground' – a track which stands up there with 'Close To The Edge', 'Karn Evil Nine' and 'Supper's Ready' in the hallowed hall of 1970s side-long prog rock monuments.

On leaving Camel, and after two decades away from producing music, soon after moving to Japan in 2003, he released two solo albums, *Full Circle* and *Into the Sun*. He still lives in the Land of the Rising Sun, releasing a number of solo albums, the most recent of which, at time of writing, being *Out Of Sinc* in 2018.

Mel Collins (Born 1947)
Flute, saxes, oboe, clarinet, piccolo 1976-1979, 1984 (guest, one concert)
Born on the Isle of Man into a musical family, Collins is best known for his work in progressive rock, first with King Crimson (*In The Wake Of Poseidon*, *Lizard*, *Islands*, *Earthbound* and *Red*), Chris Squire (*Fish Out Of Water*) and the Alan Parsons Project (*Eye In The Sky*). Collins' flexibility means he's able to play in variety of styles ranging from R&B and blues-rock to pop and jazz, making him a sought-after session player, responsible for some of pop and rock's most memorable sax solos, including those on 'Let's Stick Together' by Bryan Ferry, 'Miss You' from the Stones and Tina Turner's 'Private Dancer'.

Collins was a feature in Camel both in the studio (*Rain Dances*, *Breathless*, *I Can See Your House From Here*, *Stationary Traveller*) and on tour for those albums, albeit only as a guest for one gig on the latter. His solo on the *A Live*

Record rendition of 'Never Let Go' adds a whole new dimension to that song, making it, in many fans' estimation, the definitive version. In 1984 Collins made his last studio contribution to Camel during the *Stationary Traveller* sessions.

Post-Camel, Mel returned to session work, including contributions to Tears for Fears' *Songs From The Big Chair* and multiple Gerry Rafferty LPs: in case you were wondering, though, it's not Collins playing sax on 'Baker Street' – his work with the Scotsman began after *City to City*. He also toured with Roger Waters in support of *The Pros and Cons of Hitchhiking*, before in 2002 joining former King Crimson men Ian McDonald, Jakko Jakszyk, Peter and Michael Giles, and Ian Wallace in forming 21st Century Schizoid Band.

In 2013, after a royal summons from Robert Fripp, Collins returned to the King Crimson mothership, where he has been ever since.

Jan Schelhaas (Born 1948)
Keyboards, 1978–1981 (touring 2013)

Born in Liverpool to a Dutch father and English mother, Jan kicked off his musical career as a bassist, playing with an assortment of local outfits from 1963 to 1965 – the height of both Merseybeat and The Cavern Club itself. In 1968 he joined soulsters Bernie and the Buzz Band, who recorded a couple of singles, and in the following year, he formed Business, a psychedelic rock band whose main *raison d'etre* was backing vocal groups like Scaffold – they of 'Lily the Pink' fame. It was this association with Scaffold that led Schelhaas to switch from bass to keyboards. In conversation with Mark Powell of Esoteric Records in 2008, Schelhaas recounted that the move to keyboards awoke his interest in writing, so from then on, the bass was put to one side.

1970 saw Schelhaas form National Head Band, with Neil Ford on guitar and future Uriah Heep drummer Lee Kerslake: the fruits of this combo was just the one album, *Albert One*, released in 1971 and produced by Yes engineer Eddie Offord.

Next up, in 1973, Schelhaas joined Gary Moore's band and played on its debut album, *Grinding Stone*, then concentrating on unattributed session work before in July 1975 being offered the job of keyboard player in Caravan. Schelhaas recorded two studio albums with Caravan, *Blind Dog At St. Dunstan's* (1976) and *Better By Far* (1977) before the band dissolved in 1978.

Newly unemployed, on the suggestion of Richard Sinclair, by then bassist with Camel, Schelhaas and David Sinclair joined Latimer and the gang for the last of the *Breathless* sessions and then to tour supporting the release. Schelhaas stayed full-time with Camel until 1981, touring and playing on *I Can See Your House From Here*, then guesting on *Nude*. Jan's final collaboration with Camel to date was joining the band on the *Retirement Sucks* tour in 2013, joining Guy LeBlanc on keys.

Caravan officially reformed in 1995, with Schelhaas back on board from 2002, recording new music and gigging regularly: his very enjoyable solo output is listed at the end of the book.

Kit Watkins (Born 1953)
Keyboards, piano, flute, clarinet. 1979-1982

Born in Virginia, USA, Watkins studied piano at home from the age of five: it helped that both his parents were piano teachers. In his teens, Watkins was drawn to rock music and became involved in local bands, playing organ, synthesizer and flute, as well as singing lead. By eighteen, his writing abilities were coming to the fore, and at university, he joined prog band Happy the Man – a reference to Goethe's *Faust* and not the 1972 Genesis single, as is usually assumed.

In 1976, Happy the Man were auditioned by Peter Gabriel; he was looking for a backing band for his solo career. They didn't get the gig, but the increased profile the audition gave them in no small way facilitated their signing of a five-year, multi-album deal with Arista Records. During its initial existence, which came to a close in 1979, Happy the Man released two albums, but without commercial success, Arista unsurprisingly decided to drop them.

At that exact time, Camel were looking for a keyboard player to replace David Sinclair, so Watkins was hired to play alongside Jan Schelhaas. After playing a full part in recording and touring *I Can See Your House From Here*, Watkins became frustrated that his writing contributions were being sidelined and he was absent from the studio for *Nude*, although he was credited for co-writing one track – 'Docks'. Nevertheless, the band convinced him to come back for the *Nude* tour in 1981 and the *Single Factor* tour in 1982, after which his association with Camel came to an end.

Post-Camel, Watkins embarked on a solo career, and over time his musical style veered away from prog into multiple other genres, including electronica, ambient, jazz, and world-fusion. *Field of View*, Kit's most recent LP released in 2019, includes a faithful cover version of 'Spirit of the Water': seems you can take the man out of Camel, but not Camel out of the man …

Colin Bass (Aka Sabah Habas Mustapha) (Born 1951)
Bass, keyboards, vocals. 1979–1981, 1984–present

It's easy to forget that Colin Bass has been bass player with Camel for a much longer time than original member, Doug Ferguson. Apart from a short sabbatical during 1982-1983, by 2021, he has been a feature of the band for 42 years.

Born in London, Bass started playing professionally in 1968 on six-string guitar with his band The Krisis. In 1970 he switched to bass and made his first professional recording with the psychedelic rock band Velvet Opera before joining 1960's chart-topping pop-soul band The Foundations on the cabaret club circuit. 1972 saw him teaming up with songwriter Ernie Graham to form Clancy, one of the original London 'pub rock' bands, a scene that included Brinsley Schwarz and Kilburn & The High Roads, and with whom he recorded two albums for Warner Bros Records, featuring some of his first original, but according to Bass, 'not very good' compositions.

In 1976 he joined the Steve Hillage Band for an extensive tour of Europe and the USA to promote *L* and in 1979, he joined Camel. Forming a strong bond with Andy Ward, in the period leading up to the *Nude* tour, the pair shared a flat in London.

From 1984 to 1992, in parallel with his work in Camel, under his *nom de bass* of Sabah Habas Mustapha, Colin was a member of 3 Mustaphas 3, the tongue-in-cheek but accomplished UK-based world music band allegedly originally from Szegerely in the Balkans (they entered the UK illegally after being smuggled across multiple borders in questionably manufactured fridges). If Borat has a favourite band – albeit not Kazakhstani – the Mustaphas are it. The Mustaphas toured globally to significant acclaim and were even adopted by the arbiter of all things cool and happening in the music world, John Peel.

In 1994, after a period in Paris directly after the *Nude* tour, Colin went to live in Berlin, where for fourteen years, he hosted a world music show on *Radio Multikulti*. That year also saw Bass take a trip to Indonesia, where over the next ten years, he was to record three solo albums with Indonesian musicians under his Mustaphas' alias. The first, *Denpasar Moon* (1994), was recorded in Jakarta and explored the local popular music style of Dangdut: the title track became a huge hit in Indonesia in the form of a cover-version by a singer from the Philippines.

Bass returned to the UK full-time in 2012, re-joining Camel for the re-recording of *Snow Goose* and subsequent tour. Aside from his wonderful bass playing, Colin's vocals are important to Camel both in the studio and live; his ability to impersonate accents while singing adds some fun character to the music – with 'Fox Hill' being his *pièce de resistance*.

Since his return to the UK in 2012, Bass has lived in the foothills of the Snowdonia mountain range in North Wales, where he has built a fully-equipped recording studio – Wild End – that is available for commercial use. As well as running the studio, since 2016 and together with his wife Katerina, he owns and manages an organic grocery store named *Health & Food* in the pretty market town of Llanwrst. Unknown to many, he once won an unofficial poll for 'The Best Eyebrows In Prog'.

David Paton (Born 1949)
Bass, vocals. 1982-1996

After a stint playing guitar for none other than The Bay City Rollers, it was as bassist and lead singer of Pilot that David Paton brought the mid-70s pop delights of 'Magic' and 'January' into the world. But it is for his time with The Alan Parsons Project that he is best known in rock circles, playing on every album from *Tales Of Mystery And Imagination* in 1976 to *Stereotomy* in 1985. It was through APP, who were recording *The Turn Of A Friendly Card* at Abbey Road at the same time as Camel were laying down *Nude*, that he came into the orbit of Latimer & Co, prefacing a fourteen-year association with

Camel. Interviewed in early 2021 by Jason Barnard of *thestrangebrew.co.uk*, Paton takes up the story:

> I met Andy Latimer in Abbey Road and he asked me if I could work on his album, but I said, 'I'm sorry, Andrew, but I just can't – I'm working flat out but keep in touch'. He kept in touch, and the next album [The Single Factor] came up and I was available to do it – and I got on great with Andrew. Musically it was fantastic – he was playing all the kind of music that I really liked and listened to when I was a lot younger, and I wanted to play that music live. So, I took that a bit further with Camel and I was with them about three years touring and singing on the albums, and when Andy went to live in the San Francisco area, I was invited out and sang on some new studio numbers then as well. 'Heroes' was a fantastic song to sing, and Andy also wanted me to play my fretless bass, which is a bit of a signature for me – so there I am, in my element.

After collaborating on *Dust And Dreams* and then *Harbour Of Tears* in 1996, Paton's time with Camel came to an end. In parallel to his work with Camel, from 1998 to 1996, Paton was a fixture on Rick Wakeman's prolific output of eleven studio albums (*Time Machine* to *Orisons*) as well as with Fish (*Internal Exile*, *Songs From The Mirror* and *Suits*).

At the time of writing, Paton's most recent recorded appearance is with Chris Rea on his 2019 opus, *One Fine Day*.

Chris Rainbow (1946-2015)

Vocals. 1982-1984

Born Christopher James Harley, in 1974 Chris took on the stage name 'Rainbow' to avoid confusion with Steve Harley of Cockney Rebel, then at the peak of his fame. After a few years as a moderately successful solo artist, releasing a few singles and albums for Polydor and then EMI, in 1979 he joined The Alan Parsons Project for *Eve*, where he remained a regular up to *Gaudi* in 1986.

As for David Paton, it was through APP that he was invited to join Camel for *The Single Factor* and subsequently *Stationary Traveller*, touring both of these as well.

Talking in 2001 to Francesco Ferrua of APP fansite, *theparsonsday*, Rainbow said of his time with Camel:

> I really enjoyed the Camel years ... 'Heart's Desire' and 'Long Goodbyes' were perfect for my style of delivery, and in particular, 'Long Goodbyes' is one of the best songs I have ever sung – it would have been a great APP track too.

After his time with Camel and APP, Rainbow (under his birth name of Harley, so most will have missed the connection) spent more time behind the mixing desk than in front of it. He produced all of Runrig's albums from *Heartland* in 1985 to *In Search Of Angels* in 1999, as well as building a studio on the Isle of Skye where KT Tunstall recorded *Acoustic Extravaganza*.

On Rainbow's untimely death of Parkinson's Disease in 2015, on his website Alan Parsons summed up this woefully under-rated singer:

> It was with great sadness that I read today of the passing of Chris Rainbow. He was an amazing talent and an integral part of The Project sound. Eric [Woolfson] and I used to call him the 'one man Beach Boys'. I will always remember his funny stories, his mimicking ability, and his hilarious catchphrases. Sessions with him were always filled with laughter. I will miss him greatly.

Ton Scherpenzeel (Born 1952)

Keyboards, accordion. 1983–1991 (session 1999, touring 2003, 2014–16)
In 1972 Ton Scherpenzeel was a founding member of under-appreciated Dutch prog band Kayak, who, although hugely popular in The Netherlands where they had a Number six hit with 'Ruthless Queen' in 1979, never broke outside of the Low Countries. Ton joined Camel on tour in 1983 and became a full member in 1984, recording *Stationary Traveller*. As well as touring in Europe and the UK, Ton subsequently played keys on both *Dust And Dreams* and *Rajaz*.

Interviewed by *ramzine.co.uk* in 2018, Ton said of his time with Camel:

> Apart from Andy Latimer's fantastic guitar playing, I think he and I share the same musical soul. There's a mysterious connection underneath that's really hard to describe. I was both amazed and honoured he asked me to play with Camel in 1983. I've done a couple of tours with them and really enjoyed them. Besides the musical joy, I found the pleasure of only having to play and not worrying about everything else that comes with keeping a band on the road.

Unfortunately, in 2016 Ton was unable to go to Japan with Camel. Colin Bass, via his Blog, takes up the story:

> It was touch-and-go – like this blog. It almost didn't happen, but thankfully it did. A short tour of Japan. Flagged up to us in late 2015, we immediately fell to discussing the practicalities, the most significant being: who would be the keyboard player? Our dear friend Ton Scherpenzeel, with whom we always have a wonderful time working, is a long-time committed non-flyer and, though he vouchsafed that he would seriously consider a long and arduous journey on the Trans-Siberian railway route, we felt had to look for someone else to take on the task.

Of course, that 'someone' was Peter Jones, more about whom in a little bit. Ton continues to lead Kayak, who in 2018 released their appropriately titled seventeenth LP, *Seventeen*. As mentioned earlier, guesting on one track, 'Ripples On The Water', is a certain Mr Andrew Latimer.

Paul Burgess (Born 1950)

Drums, percussion. 1983-1994

Best known for his association with 10cc, Burgess joined them on their 1973 UK tour and officially became drummer, percussionist and occasional keyboardist in 1976 after the departure of Kevin Godley and Lol Creme. His first studio album with the band was *Deceptive Bends*, which featured the hit 'The Things We Do for Love'.

After a brief stint touring with Jethro Tull in 1982, Burgess left 10cc in 1983 and joined Camel, staying for one studio album – *Stationary Traveller*, and one live album – *Pressure Points*, before the band went on hiatus in 1985.

Following Camel's 'lost years', Burgess came back to record *Dust And Dreams* and featured on the subsequent live album, *Never Let Go*.

More recently, as a result of his involvement with Magna Carta, Burgess has collaborated with Steeleye Span alumni Rick Kemp and Ken Nicol in the imaginatively named Burgess, Nicol and Kemp folk-rock 'supergroup'.

Mickey Simmonds (Born 1959)

Keyboards. 1992-1996

Mickey Simmonds was born in Chesterfield, England and remains an in-demand session keyboardist, arranger and composer. Simmonds toured with Camel following the *Dust And Dreams* release in 1992, with his performances captured on the *Never Let Go* live album (1993). Mickey joined Camel in the studio for *Harbour of Tears*, but did not tour the album, with Foster 'Foss' Patterson taking on keyboard duties.

As well as playing with Camel, he is best known for his work with progressive rock acts Renaissance and Fish. In the case of the former, check out his playing on *Tuscany* – especially 'One Thousand Roses'; with the latter, Simmonds co-wrote all but one track on Fish's 1990 solo debut *Vigil In A Wilderness Of Mirrors* and also co-wrote all tracks on the follow-up album *Internal*. Fish described him as the 'musical director' of his early solo years – quite an accolade to receive from The Big Man.

Dave Stewart (Born 1972)

Drums, percussion. 1996-1999

Prior to joining Camel, Scottish drummer and percussionist Dave Stewart worked with artists including The Blue Nile, Deacon Blue and Fish. Dave joined the band to rehearse in 1996, ahead of the *Harbour of Tears* tour the following year. He stayed to record *Rajaz*, but immediately ahead of the tour for that album, he handed in his resignation, preferring to take on the role of managing a drum shop. This new role in retail didn't prevent him from continuing his relationship with Fish, playing on all the studio albums from *Suits* in 1994 to *Fellini Days* in 2001.

After a period living in the English Midlands, Dave is now based in Edinburgh, operating as a session drummer for a number of labels, including Sony and Chrysalis.

Foster 'Foss' Patterson (Born 1955)
Keyboards, backing vocals. 1996-1997
Best known as keyboard player for fellow Scots, John Martyn and Fish, he is also a vocalist, composer, arranger and in-demand session keyboardist, working with a dizzying range of artists around the world. He has produced work for movies and TV, plus commercials and incidental and soundtrack music for the *BBC*, *Discovery Channel*, and other channels and networks.

Along with fellow Fish band alumnus, Dave Stewart, Foss toured with Camel on the *Harbour of Tears* tour in 1997, but unlike Stewart was not around for the recording of *Rajaz* in 1999. Foss continues to tour and record with Fish and has been an almost-ever-present feature since *Songs From The Mirror* in 1993 to 2020's *Weltschmerz*, with only a brief sabbatical for the recordings of *Fellini Days* and *Field Of Crows*.

Guy LeBlanc (1960-2015)
Keyboards, vocals. 2000-2014
Born in 1960 in New Brunswick, Canada, LeBlanc began formal musical training at age four, ending his classical piano training at eleven in order to concentrate on composition and modern electric music. He started playing keyboards in rock bands at fifteen and co-founded prog-fusion band Nathan Mahl when he was twenty: quite the prodigy!

Guy joined Camel in 1999, touring extensively during 2000 and 2001, playing keyboards on *A Nod And A Wink* and then the re-recording of *Snow Goose* in 2013.

Although desperate to tour with the band in 2014, his bandmates and Hoover saw how ill he was and persuaded him to rest: Ton Scherpenzeel, not for the first time, stepped in at the last minute. Guy was clearly dismayed to not be joining the band, as his message to fans at the time underlined:

One of the greatest joys of my life was the opportunity to join Camel for the comeback / 'Retirement Sucks' tour of 2013. The whole thing was an amazing experience; performing this music for all the wonderful people who came to all the shows. The positive emotions felt throughout transcended mere words, and the camaraderie and joviality within the band and crew still evokes smiles from my lips on a daily basis.

I'm so glad that Ton has agreed to do this, and also very relieved. It saddens me deeply that I will not see my friends, but the love and support I've received gives me strength and I look forward to seeing everyone again once this hurdle is passed.

Sadly, that 'hurdle' wasn't passed, Guy didn't recover and his time with the band was tragically to be cut short. In 2015, another Camel keyboard player was lost to cancer.

Denis Clement (Born 1971)
Drums, percussion, recorder, arrangements. 2000-
French-Canadian Denis Clement joined Camel just ten days before their first show of the 'Y2k' Tour, replacing previous drummer Dave Stewart who, for reasons best known to himself, opted to manage a drum store in his native Scotland instead of staying with the band.

Prior to his continuing association with Camel, Denis was the drummer for the Steve Groves Trio and Canada's answer to Level 42, Spyral Jones. Clement's drum style is clearly reminiscent of Andy Ward, with some real punch, intricate cymbal work and fast fills: his character and enthusiasm behind the kit are infectious.

But he's not a one-trick pony: when the band play 'Spirit Of The Water', he'll whip out his recorder or keyboard to duet with Latimer – no taking a break during a drum-free song for our Denis.

Peter Jones (Born 1980)
Keyboards, saxophone, pennywhistle, vocals. 2016-
Supremely talented multi-instrumentalist Pete Jones lost his sight at fifteen months due to retinoblastoma. From an early age, he was into all things musical and, at the age of four, had his first piano.

Pete studied music and music technology, and over time his writing style moved more into a conventional pop genre, though he experimented with many styles, both modern and classical. In 2010 Pete had his first official album release with *Look At Me Now*; this self-penned and produced album was a collection of songs from the previous ten years, spanning multiple genres but with an overall contemporary AOR feel.

In 2013 Pete, under the moniker of Tiger Moth Tales – a reference to Steve Hackett's song from *Spectral Mornings* – released *Cocoon*, a concept album on the subject of childhood, and coming to terms with its loss. Pete says of the album:

It all happened by accident, really. One day I sat down to try and write a song and ended up with the beginning of a prog song about a children's TV show. I had no idea what I was going to do with it, but as I tried to focus more on conventional music, I kept getting more and more ideas about songs on childhood subjects, and in my head, it was all prog. It seemed there was nothing for it but to see the thing through and see what happened.

The prog and rock press were fulsome in their praise, and as a result of this raised profile and a personal recommendation, Pete was approached to join

Camel for the 2016 trip to Japan (Ton Scherpenzeel being unable to participate due to his aforementioned fear of flying). A rehearsal room was booked in Jones' home city of Nottingham: when I spoke with Colin Bass in 2021, he vividly recalled:

> I can remember that day very well. Denis came over from Canada, and as Pete was setting up, we were all thinking: 'He's playing this old Technics keyboard and everything's on a floppy disk: what?!' But right there and then, we were dumbfounded: Pete had learned to program it and got a great Hammond sound. We were amazed he could get those sounds out of that thing. We all stayed and did another week of rehearsals for the Japanese tour.

Pete's instrumental and improvisational talents have brought a new dynamism to Camel's live performances: as well as singing, he stuns audiences with his extended alto sax solo during *Rajaz* – a definite highlight of recent gigs.

As well as his touring duties with Camel, Pete continues to release albums as Tiger Moth Tales with critically acclaimed LPs *Cocoon*, *Depths of Winter*, *Still Alive* and *The Whispering Of The World*, all selling well in the progressive rock community.

Susan Hoover

Lyricist, manager. 1976-
Andrew Latimer met US-born broadcast journalist and DJ Susan Hoover when the band were interviewed on her KSJO San Jose radio show in 1976. Andy shared the story with me early in 2021:

> She interviewed the band in 1976 at The Boarding House in San Francisco, but apparently, the tape was the legal copyright of the radio station and was only aired once. We hit it off and were married in 1979. When I got out of the Decca contract in 1986, we decided to handle the business ourselves and called it DIY Management; after a fateful meeting with an A&R man at Virgin Records, we were inspired to set up our own label and that was the catalyst for the move to the USA.

Susan contributed to the lyrics early on and became full-time lyricist in 1984 with *Stationary Traveller*. Even though she deliberately keeps a low profile, Susan is a vital driving force behind Camel and remains Latimer's muse. After the return to the UK in 2006, Andy and Susan live together in the countryside of beautiful Wiltshire in the South West of England.

Album Covers

Unlike, say, Yes who are synonymous with Roger Dean's fantasy art, or Pink Floyd's association with graphic designers Hipgnosis, Camel's record sleeves have no contiguous theme or design elements that would immediately identify an LP with the band should there be a new release poster in the window of your local record store. Nor does the band have an identifiable logo à la Rush's 'Starman' or, of course, Yes: with the exception of *Mirage* and *Snow Goose*, every other studio album has a different styling of 'Camel'. In fact, pretty much every cover is radically different from what went before: line up your copies and behold!

This lack of a theme wasn't a conscious decision; it just sort of happened, with the band each time electing to go with a cover that related directly to the content or concept of the album in question. Overall, we do end up with a rather eclectic mix of styles which, with the exception of *Moonmadness*, don't really add to the artform of 70s progressive rock LP sleeves or indeed that genre in general: for Camel, it's all about the music.

In the case of *Mirage*, there are two different sleeves as a result of the putative legal action by Camel cigarettes in the USA: more about that later in the book. The US sleeve is a nightmarish creation straight out of a bad trip: a dragon with a camel's head – it's hideous.

Moonmadness also had a different cover for the US release, a bone of contention amongst fans and band alike (although it did spawn the camel-in-a-spacesuit watercolour, which over time has become somewhat of an icon, appearing ubiquitously on T-shirts and other merchandise). The UK and 'rest of the world' sleeve was a gatefold thing of beauty, painted by John Field: speaking to *Prog* magazine in 2019, Latimer said:

> Our record company asked several designers to come up with an album sleeve. The instructions were that it would be called Moonmadness and, as it was in those days – and I can remember Pink Floyd talking about The Dark Side Of The Moon and it was the same thing – they just had a title and the designers came in with various ideas. The band looked at them and we all agreed that we liked this one by Field. It was pretty rare that we all agreed on anything, but it was such a great cover. We didn't work directly with Field as his design was so good – why change it?

I Can See Your House From Here, due to controversy around the crucified astronaut on the main release, likewise birthed a separate LP cover, this time in South Africa, copies of which are much sought-after by Camel completists; the cover itself is a bit of a mess, comprising a rather second-rate sci-fi painting.

Pardon the mixed metaphor; the band didn't flog a dead horse with the camel thing either. In total, only four out of the fourteen studio albums (fifteen if you count the re-recorded *Snow Goose*) have one or multiple camels on the front cover – five if you count the USA Janus release of *Moonmadness*.

My personal favourite, though, is *Nude*, with its Belgian cartoonist-surrealist, Hergé meets Magritte mash-up: the 'empty suit' inference doesn't really work in the context of Hiroo Onoda, but it's a cool piece of artwork all the same.

Above: MCA throws some cash behind promoting the debut album, sadly to little avail with the buying public. (*Private collection of Shane Carlson*)

Camel (1973)

Personnel:
Andrew Latimer: guitar, vocals
Peter Bardens: keyboards, vocals
Doug Ferguson: bass, vocals
Andy Ward: drums, percussion
Produced by Dave Williams at Morgan Studios, London, 15–26 August 1972
Engineer: Roger Quested
Release date: 28 February 1973
Running time: 39:17
Current edition: MCA CD 8829252
Highest Chart Places: did not chart

Under the wings of the Gemini Artists (GAMA), now spearheaded by Max Hole as well as founder Geoff Jukes, Camel signed to MCA in August 1972. Hole's claim to fame at this point was his coup of booking The Who for the then scary sum of £1,000, but still managing to make a profit of £150; Jukes was a booker for Chrysalis Records: they were a perfect fit for the boys. As for Hole, well, aside from in 2013 becoming chairman and CEO of Universal Music Group International, on his retirement in 2015, he was awarded the CBE by Prince Charles: the boy done good.

Anyway, this one-album deal, with an option for a second and third, came about mainly as a consequence of Bardens' pedigree – he had, after all, worked with some heavyweight names, including Rod Stewart, Van Morrison, Peter Green and Mick Fleetwood – albeit all of them before they hit the big time.

Camel was recorded at Morgan Studios in North London over eleven days in August 1972. The band were in illustrious company: other albums recorded there around that time included *A Passion Play* (Jethro Tull), *Tales from Topographic Oceans* (Yes), *Billion Dollar Babies* (Alice Cooper) and *Sabbath Bloody Sabbath* (Black Sabbath), so it's clear that MCA had high hopes and were willing to invest.

Dave Williams, the producer, was less than complimentary regarding the band's vocal talents and thus, midway through the sessions, the band embarked on a wild goose chase. They auditioned some 40-odd singers over three days and when interviewed by *Prog* magazine in 2018, Latimer said '…They were all awful': Williams had to defer, unwittingly cementing the band's belief that although they knew they weren't the best vocalists in town, their very English and melancholic tones were right for the type of music Camel were writing. Over the coming LPs, Latimer, Bardens and Ferguson shared vocal duties, and another trademark was stamped on the Camel sound. Latimer, on *CV* says of this decision:

A lasting effect of deciding to carry on with our own vocals was that we kept them low in the mix and used effects like Leslie, phasing, chorusing, echo – all sorts of things to bury them, in a way.

Engineered by Roger Quested, who already had Led Zeppelin, Pink Floyd and Cat Stevens on his CV, like many debut albums, it's a little disjointed and occasionally rough around the edges. Even though Morgan's set up was unquestionably state-of-the-art for the time, in places, the recording technology lets the music down, with an overall 'clipped' or compressed sonic spectrum that compromises the band's already wide dynamic range and varying textures. In particular, the Hammond organ sound seems to be straining the capabilities of the microphones and mixing desk, and the bass often sounds muffled. But these are minor quibbles and it could be argued that this only adds to the authenticity of a band on its first steps to legendary status.

However, the label didn't get quite what it hoped for – which, unsurprisingly at the time, was radio-ready, hummable hits that might pass the 'Old Grey Whistle Test'. Instead, and to the eternal credit of the band, it got a coherent musical manifesto from musicians itching to break away from the confines of three-minute pop songs and explore the possibilities of the relatively new world of progressive rock. After mediocre first-year sales of around 5,000 units, and a spring clean of its roster, MCA didn't take up the option for a second LP. Latimer said on *CV*: '*Camel* was a mishmash of material – we didn't have a direction', with Bardens adding, more positively:

It hadn't totally evolved into the style of music it was to become, but it was a worthy effort. In fact, listening to it now in 1993, all these years later, it has a little bit of a Santana-y feel to it, which I kinda like. It was heavy on the soloing and it still stands up as a good album.

Soon after the release of *Camel* in 1973, the band did a live session for John Peel on BBC Radio 1, and after a couple of seconds of silence, his closing remarks bear repeating:

You can always tell when I'm enjoying a programme, 'cos I never work out what I'm going to say in between pieces of music, and this is one such: that was Camel and 'Never Let Go' – pretty original, and I like it.

Soon after, however, he ghosted them in favour of more avant-garde material. Such was his apparent change of heart that during a 1985 British Forces Broadcasting Service show, he became borderline apoplectic when a listener told him that the first half of one of his programmes in Cologne had been cancelled due to a Camel gig happening the same night. This was, he said, 'the ultimate indignity' and called them 'a gang of clapped-out old hippies'. This story has a coda: in 2012, eight years after his death, four Camel albums – *Camel, The Snow Goose, Moonmadness* and *Rain Dances* were found among his personal record collection: it seems that in his case at least, an old hippie really didn't die.

'Slow Yourself Down' (Latimer, Ward)

Given the time and place, 'Slow Yourself Down' is a great opener, showcasing the band's full talents in a shade under five minutes. It's all here if you care to look for it: wonderful Hammond work, walking bass lines, swinging drum work and, of course – after keeping his powder dry for the first two minutes, Latimer's melodic wig-out that leads into an epic instrumental peaking with perfectly unison guitar and keys supported by a driving backbeat: when this gets going with a rattle of toms and a perfectly judged guitar twang, it's magic.

As alluded to above, this is no three-minute pop song, borne out by the unusual song structure, sparing vocals and instrumentation that calls to mind Traffic at their best, particularly in the middle eight. For such an uplifting number, the melancholic vocal counterpoint that was to become a band trademark throughout its life, marks out Camel as something new and unique, instead of simply being a downer.

'Mystic Queen' (Bardens)

The down-tempo intro immediately suggests psychedelia – think Mamas & Papas or Jefferson Airplane – and the rest of the song doesn't stray far from this vibe: mystic, indeed.

Opening with some lovely, atmospheric acoustic guitar from Latimer, it's Bardens' work here that's a masterclass in using the dynamics of the Hammond to weave in and out of a lead role in friendly competition with Latimer's switches between the aforementioned acoustic and then electric guitar. The number closes with a glissando guitar coda, double-tracked over acoustic, that's straight out of the Steve Hillage playbook and is an early indication both of Latimer's melodic and technical virtuosity, as well as his ability to seamlessly switch between guitar styles in a single song.

As for 'Curiosity' later in the LP, Ferguson takes up the (yet again, sparse) vocal duties, acquitting himself well.

'Six Ate' (Latimer)

From the off, the band weren't afraid to stray from 4/4, 'common time' tunes, and 'Six Ate' swings, baby! 'Six Ate', of course, references the 6/8 time signature and as the first instrumental in the Camel catalogue, it's a statement of intent that the band wasn't going to be a purely lyric-based outfit. Here we see the band's jazz/fusion leanings in sharp focus for the first time, and as we'll see further down the catalogue, these tracks are often the most musically accomplished of the band's output. Bardens sits way back in the mix until a snappy synth solo pops out front. According to the sleeve notes, apart from Hammond, the only other keyboards were piano and Mellotron, with a VCS3 for effects (as best heard on 'Arubaluba' later), so I'm a little puzzled as this solo sounds just like a Minimoog, of which there was certainly at least one on-hand at Morgan.

'Separation' (Latimer)
Separation fairly gallops out of the starting gate and just keeps on going to the finish line, pausing only to take a dreamy breather halfway through. The speed of the lyrics is almost punky in its intensity and the song packs in a lot in just under four minutes. The rhythm & blues influences of the musicians' early work is a clear underpinning: there's lots of fun along the way, with a sustained guitar wig out to close. In summation, it's not exactly the sort of overture one might expect to the next track on the album.

'Never Let Go' (Latimer)
So far in the debut effort, so 'fair enough': and then this – the first unquestioned Camel classic and a live staple-cum-fan favourite ever since. It's the moment when we glimpse the possibilities – and it's quite a vista. That 12-string riff (fans of Opeth may recognise 'Benighted', which is based on this); those hope-filled lyrics; those textbook Camel dynamic and tempo shifts. Layer all this with more of the inspired interplay between Bardens and Latimer, more than ably supported by Ferguson's funky fretwork (brought forward in the mix with the remaster, and rightly so) and Ward's jazz-flecked fills.

There's an immediate maturity of songwriting and arranging, here, that marks out 'Never Let Go' as the unquestioned highlight of the record; that's not to say that the other tracks aren't up to scratch, just that this one stands out so clearly, delivering a melodic prog masterpiece.

'Never Let Go' features Bardens for the first time at the mic, and so at this stage in the LP, we've had all three vocalists on duty. Maybe Williams was onto something insofar as none of the three were singers in the vein of Steve Winwood, Robert Plant, Peter Gabriel or many of the other lauded frontmen of the time, with the engineer processing the vocals in almost every instance to compensate. But this is surely missing the point: each of Camel's three bring something special to the overall sound, and the fact that they seamlessly interchange from number to number – sometimes unidentifiably – gave the band a versatility that many peers didn't have.

'Never Let Go' was released as the band's first single, with 'Curiosity' as the B-Side, but it didn't chart. Later in the song's life, the inclusion of sax and synths serve only to make it even better – as evidenced on the *A Live Record* version. For many – including myself – this was the 'free first hit' or gateway drug that led to a Camel addiction. Simply magnificent.

'Curiosity' (Bardens)
The songwriting credits on *Camel* are pretty evenly split between Latimer and Bardens, but interestingly no track on this album is jointly written. As such, there aren't any clues as to the later emergence of the joint Latimer/ Bardens writing that makes up not only the bulk of the tunes that were to come later in the Bardens-era catalogue but also the band's best-loved tracks from this period.

Sadly, 'Curiosity' is probably the weakest track on the record, an ambling somewhat disposable ditty that doesn't fit the overall mood of the album, and frankly doesn't say much of import about the band either, so it's odd that it was chosen as the B-side of the 'Never Let Go' single release. Nevertheless, we're left in no doubt who the stars were going to be: Bardens' Hammond takes centre stage, and Latimer gives his pedal board a proper workout with at least three different effects in evidence.

'Arubaluba' (Bardens)

With its use of Arabian pentatonics, album closer 'Arubaluba' is the first time we hear the band's Levantine leanings that would come to the fore on *Mirage* – as well as Bardens having some jolly fun twisting the knobs, twiddling the joystick and poking the patch pegs of a VCS3 Synth.

It's 'Arubaluba' that really sets out the idea that Camel would be classed as a prog and not a straight rock act, not only because of the synth bubbles and whooshes but also due to the complex time signatures and the interplay between keys and guitar. The first few bars give no indication at all of the groove that's coming – another indication of the nascent compositional talent and ability to surprise that the band would develop over the coming years. In total, there are eight distinct passages to the piece. Eight!

Again, we can hear the influence of Traffic both in the wailing guitar work and the overdriven Hammond that was a trademark of Winwood and the gang. As for Ward's drumming, well – wow. The remaster really brings him forward in the mix, and it's a joy to hear. As a transition from *Camel* to *Mirage*, you might think that the band already had 'Freefall' in mind when they chose to end with 'Arubaluba' …

Associated Tracks
'Homage To The God Of Light' (Bardens)

(Recorded Live at The Marquee Club – 29 October 1974)

This song appeared on Barden's 1971 LP *The Answer* and now extended in a live setting from the original thirteen minutes, could well have been named 'Nineteen Minutes Of Needless Narcissistic Noodling', but it stands as an interesting historical artefact all the same.

At the 14-minute mark, we again hear Latimer's lovely glissando work, this time backed by more VCS3 pops, bubbles, whooshes and squeaks. It's real jam band stuff, this, which is no bad thing (think Grateful Dead, Little Feat and Phish), but I suspect many a bathroom break was taken in the Marquee's legendarily dodgy lavatories and many a pint purchased, during its almost twenty-minute onslaught.

Nevertheless, given the date of recording and the venue, it's likely that on the night, this extended structured improv went down a treat. It's properly *Meddle*-era Floyd in places and was a fixture of the live set in the early years. This is understandable, one supposes, given the limited catalogue back then. I do have a problem, though, with its inclusion on the remaster as chronologically it was recorded during the *Mirage* tour, and therefore I think it would have been better placed on the extended release of that album. On balance, as an addition to the 2002 remaster, it's better included than not.

Wonderfully for us fans, the last thing we hear is the compère wishing the band 'the best of luck in The States', a reference to the first US tour, predominantly as support for Wishbone Ash, which kicked off on 19 November 1974 at Ladyland in New York City. Our heroes' occidental escapades, which, due to their warm reception, continued beyond the originally planned December end date, culminated with a gig at the Long Beach Arena in California on 17 January 1975. Also on the bill that night, sandwiched between Camel and Wishbone Ash, was a nascent Kiss: there's a piece of Pub Quiz trivia for the ages. Almost immediately after returning to London, Camel were in Basing Street Studios recording *The Snow Goose* – but we're jumping ahead. Next up in our story is *Mirage*.

Mirage (1974)

Personnel:
Andrew Latimer: guitar, vocals
Peter Bardens: keyboards, vocals
Doug Ferguson: bass, vocals
Andy Ward: drums, percussion
Produced by David Hitchcock at Island Studios (Basing Street Studios), London,
November 1973
Release date: 1 March 1974.
Running time: 38:22
Current edition: Deram CD 8829292
Highest chart places: did not chart

By the second album, not only were the band gelling as a unit, the signature
Camel sound was really starting to emerge – that smoky cocktail of the exotic
and the pastoral, and with it, they delivered an unquestionable prog rock
classic.

Also, it was the band's first brush with legal problems. The cover's
resemblance to the cigarette brand of the same name is somewhat obvious,
and this was enough to incur the wrath of the parent company's lawyers
in the USA. As ever with Camel, things were a little more complicated, as
management (in the person of Jukes) had already struck an (according to Ward
'shady' ...) deal with the European subsidiary of the tobacco company to give
away mini, five cig packets as a promotion. As they say, 'the bloody road to Hell
is paved with good intentions ...' So enthused, in fact, was the company that
it sent reps to some of the studio sessions, with the inevitable consequence
of starting to interfere in the creative process by suggesting name changes to
songs that would be more in-line with the cigarette theme. The salespeople
even suggested draping the amps in camel skins: don't ask. Anyway, all's well
that ends well and all that, so with a swift cover re-design of the US release, the
lawyers were back in their box.

Moving back to the music, the leap forward in compositional maturity
compared with the first album is startling. Whereas most of the tracks
on the debut album were more-or-less straightforward melodically and
instrumentation-wise, on *Mirage* Camel's extended, multi-movement, almost
symphonic structures are introduced. Also, for the first time, we hear Latimer's
unquestionable talents as a flautist, adding further texture that helps define
the quintessential Camel sound. In fact, it could be argued that the addition of
flute to the repertoire was a touch of unwitting promotional genius, given that
at this point in time, only four other 'name' bands broadly in the progressive
genre, Focus, Traffic, Genesis and of course Jethro Tull with Ian Anderson, used
the instrument to any significant degree, thus marking out Camel as something
special. Bardens also extended his *batterie de musique*, adding Minimoog to
the mix, resulting in some real head-turning moments.

As stated earlier, MCA didn't exercise its option for a second LP, so while the band were already in Island Records' Basing Street Studios in Notting Hill, funded at Gama's expense, Jukes negotiated a long-term, ten record deal with Decca Records for Camel and the rest of the Gama stable. Decca's 'Deram' imprint was regarded as the first of the British progressive labels and home to The Moody Blues, Giles, Giles & Fripp and Egg, so the association further cemented Camel's genre credentials.

Recording took place in November 1973, and as the majority of the new material had been played and perfected on the road, this made for a stress-free experience in the studio resulting in an album with 'clarity and direction'. Mixing and post-production was also swift, and the album was released on March 1, 1974, to critical acclaim, but not – at that stage – sales commensurate with the plaudits.

'Freefall' (Bardens)
With its atmospheric 'white noise' wind effects, crescendo-ing synth and pulsating bass intro, from the off, we know we're heading in a far more progressive direction than anything on the first album. This is the first time we hear the Eastern influences that were to become occasional but vital elements of the Camel sound and, importantly, we also get a glimpse of the multi-movement songwriting style typical of much of the band's output from here on. The classic 'Lady Fantasy', this album's closer, is also being a prime example of the form.

Lyrically, comprising only a couple of short verses and a reprise, there's nothing profound to be uncovered here. In fact, the subject matter is a run-of-the-mill and clichéd early-70s ode to the pleasures of marijuana, and the vocals – although certainly distinctive and subject to a degree of processing – act more as punctuation than narrative.

Once we're past the singing, the next section is a driving jam featuring Latimer's increasingly intricate guitar, with only a hint of Hammond from Bardens towards the end, followed by a beautifully melodic modulated middle-eight that leads us back into the reprise of both the vocals and the intro, bookending this seminal and uplifting number: the caravanserai has now really begun.

'Supertwister' (Bardens)
Enter the flute! Nothing that the band recorded to this point gave any clue either to its imminent inclusion or how vital this instrument would be to Camel's trademark sound. And it's fabulous.

Only subtly evident in the opening bars, and to today's ears likely assumed to be a string synth, after a jaunty jig with organ and bass, we hear Latimer's talent as a flautist in full swing. Yet again, the song follows a multi-movement format with a sublime, lilting middle section.

Camel were fans of the heavily Canterbury-influenced Netherlands band Supersister, who also had flute as part of their sound and the track is certainly in the same syncopated vein of much of that band's output. So, 'Supertwister' is a tribute to the Dutchmen, whose catalogue is well worth seeking out.

Given what was to come, maybe a Champagne cork popping at the end would have been more appropriate, but a can of – presumably Dutch – beer will have to do. It's a tad over three minutes long, but oh boy, what a three minutes it is – a Camel cameo, in miniature and perfect.

'Nimrodel' / 'The Procession' / 'The White Rider' (Latimer)

Before the production of the Peter Jackson movies in the 2000s, the first heyday of *Lord of the Rings* fandom was the 1970s, so it's perhaps unsurprising that Camel's first concept piece takes the Tolkien books as its subject matter.

Nimrodel was an elf-maid and lived near a river that would later take her name, and this liquid association is represented by a languid, fluid instrumental introduction on organ and synths lasting under a minute. 'The Procession' does pretty much what it says on the box, with martial snare drum – as we'll see later, a particular favourite of Andy Ward – fife-a-like flute accompaniment and muted crowd sound effects, only some 50 seconds in length. All of the above acts as a prelude for the main event: 'The White Rider', or Gandalf, as he's better known these days.

There's a lovely but brief oboe or possibly Cor Anglais figure early on, but exactly what instrument this is remains a mystery as neither of these are credited on the sleeve. The Mellotron did have an oboe setting, but to say that this sounded in any way like the actual instrument would be a real stretch, so annoyingly, we're left wondering both who? and what? Anyway, that puzzle put to one side, 'The White Rider' section makes up the bulk of the track and is a musical sketch of the wizard's character. There are multiple motifs and although this was written by Latimer alone, Bardens really lets loose on the Minimoog around the halfway point before guitar and vocals come to the fore.

The lyrics, in not very sophisticated rhyming couplets, tell the (very) potted history of Gandalf's mystical journey from Grey to White, with the smattering of flying horses and distant stars required in any self-respecting fantasy song. It gets very proggy in the final third, with Latimer's Echoplexed guitar sounding all the world like Steve Howe's pedal steel on 'Going For The One' three years before that was committed to tape. All in all, this number, more than any before it, represents the shape of things to come.

'Earthrise' (Bardens, Latimer)

Earthrise is the famous picture of our planet taken by Apollo 8 astronaut William Anders in 1968. Over the years, it has been an inspiration for musicians as diverse as classical wind ensembles, jazz bands and choirs. Camel beat them all to the punch with this.

Lifting off gently with some spacey effects, wind chimes and heavily reverbed acoustic guitar and organ, we're lulled into thinking this will be an ethereal journey calling to mind the vastness of space and the insignificance of our pale blue dot. The next two minutes do nothing to dispel the illusion with its lovely lilting Moog passage, then some fun call & response between Moog and Hammond. Then Bam! we're off on a double – then triple-time – rocket ride.

Andy Ward's drum work is a real feature on this track – it feels like he's finally been let off the leash, throwing funk-inspired fills here, there and everywhere, acting more as a distinct instrumentalist than merely being there to hold the beat; it's truly liberating to properly hear his chops for the first time. Although forceful and complicated, and with the inherent danger of overshadowing the lead instruments, the drums manage to seamlessly integrate with the rest of the band resulting in a feeling of astonishing tightness and empathy between the musicians that continues for another four-and-a-half minutes of frenetic synth and guitar interplay.

Bardens and Latimer seemingly push the boundaries further on each subsequent bar: the distorted Hammond calls to mind *The Master*, Jon Lord, in all his glory, and Latimer's soaring Santana-inspired soloing is masterful.

Strangely given how clearly all the other instruments sound, even on the remaster, the bass is muddy and buried deep in the mix, which is a real shame because if you listen very, very carefully, Ferguson's fingers are running up and down the fretboard like banshees.

The song ends on a down-tempo note with a slight variation on the original theme, rounding off a number that is as epic and uplifting as its subject matter. 'Earthrise' is a real eye-opener into the woefully underappreciated technical mastery of Camel, and coming so early in the catalogue, I am sure, was a key moment in turning on the music press to their talents.

'Lady Fantasy' (Bardens, Latimer, Ward, Ferguson)

If 'Never Let Go' is the key track on Camel, there's no question whatsoever that 'Lady Fantasy' is the cornerstone of *Mirage*. That's not to diminish one iota the quality of the rest of the album, which was, after all, voted no. 51 in the Top 100 Prog Albums of All Time by readers of *Prog* magazine in 2014, but nevertheless, this song merits *magnum opus* status, and justifiably so. A multi-section tour-de-force of songwriting and musicianship, 'Lady Fantasy' ticks all the Camel boxes present and future. At a tad under thirteen minutes long, it never outstays its welcome as the dynamic and melodic shifts are addictive and leave the listener powerless to resist. It could be twice as long, and I don't think anyone would object as there's so much going on.

Right from the first bars, with that now-famous and inimitable organ arpeggio, tom rolls and portentous A minor-key guitar riff, there's no doubt there's something special on the way – it's in your face alright, and some. It's such a clever compositional device because at the 47-second mark, what might have been expected to continue in a vein of Wagnerian bombast switches tempo and dynamics into a 30-second melodic passage prefacing the main theme of 'Encounter', the first section of this three-part work. What a way to kick off a number.

'Encounter' carries on with that unforgettable guitar melody that segues into some lovely harmonic interplay between guitar and keys, then just when we think we're heading on an even keel, there's another change of metre. The quality and critically, maturity of composition here is astounding, mind-bending, even considering how early we are in the story. So much has happened in the previous minute-and-change, and there's still eleven more to go! 'Listen very carefully, my words are about to unfold...concerning a lady I've seen, but I never could hold' – lyrics that every Camel follower has imprinted on their soul. What we have here is musical storytelling on a different level, words and instruments perfectly aligned. Nevertheless, Andy Ward, quoted in 2018 on the *Musicaficianado* blog, was not beyond a bit of self-criticism:

> I think the lyrics to that are absolutely dreadful, and I wrote some of them... when you compare them to a songwriter who's really got something to say.

'Smiles For You', the shortest of the three sections, acts as an instrumental bridge and is essentially a Latimer solo showcase backed by some wonderfully funky left-hand organ playing and a driving rhythm section. As the solo reaches its peak, the panning from left to right is sure to bring a smile: sometimes, it's the simple things, and not over-engineering, that work the best.

And now, the main event: 'Lady Fantasy' itself. In six distinct parts, we're treated to a banquet of restrained keyboards, double-tracked guitars (electric to the fore and acoustic sitting quietly but vitally in the back of the mix), clean bass and precision drumming. The soloing is transcendent – a pinch of glissando, precisely controlled feedback panning across the speakers and Latimer's legendary touch. Vocal duties are shared between Bardens and Latimer, who sing some gorgeous harmonies, underlining 'Lady Fantasy' as a love song for the ages. The boys, they themselves admitted, were not the greatest of singers and received more than their share of detractors in the studio. In the same 2018 *Musicaficianado* post, Ward commented:

> Vocally the band were weak compared, say to Caravan, who had two great singers, Pye Hastings and Richard Sinclair, two terrific singers. Pete and Andy didn't have that, and they knew this to be true; it was hard for them, but at least they gave it a go.

To my mind, however, Camel wouldn't be Camel without them, and on this showing, though, I fail to see what all the fuss was about.

'Lady Fantasy' finishes as it started, firstly with a heavy-as-you-like organ-led wig-out and then reprising the theme of 'Encounter'. Everything is so *right* that the last seven minutes seemingly go in a flash. Two albums in and Camel have progressed further than even they might have imagined at the time, delivering a masterpiece of truly progressive rock, plain and simple. 'Lady Fantasy' has more than any other song been Camel's chosen concert encore since 1984, underlining its magic. I can't wait to hear it live once more.

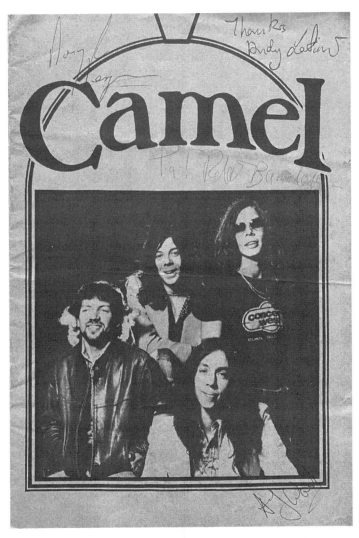

Above: The boys looking properly chuffed on the cover of the programme for the *Moonmadness* tour in 1976. (*Private collection of Shane Carlson*)

Music Inspired By The Snow Goose (1975)
Original recording
Personnel:
Andrew Latimer: guitar, vocals
Peter Bardens: keyboards, vocals
Doug Ferguson: bass, vocals
Andy Ward: drums, percussion
Produced by David Hitchcock at Island Studios (Basing Street Studios) / Decca
Studios (post-production), London.
Release date: April 1975
Running time: 43:05
Current edition: Decca CD 8829302
Highest chart places: UK: 22 USA: 162

The Snow Goose (2013)
Re-recorded version
Personnel:
Andrew Latimer: guitar, flute, keyboards, vocals
Guy LeBlanc: keyboards, vocals
Colin Bass: bass, vocals
Denis Clement: drums, percussion, keyboards
Produced by Andy Latimer and Denis Clement
Release date: May 2013.
Running time: 49:59
Current edition: Camel Productions CP0014CD
Highest chart places: None

...or The Snow *Geese*, one might say, as there's three distinct CD versions
to choose from: the original 1975 studio version, the live Royal Albert Hall
version (also 1975) included on *A Live Record* and then the 2013 re-recorded
studio version with the Latimer, LeBlanc, Clement and Bass line-up, as well
as a fourth complete run-through with the 2013 *In From The Cold* DVD
performance. This is the record that brought the band a worldwide audience
– and more legal controversy. In the early days, it seems the band had an
almost magnetic ability for piquing the interest of lawyers: oh, what innocent
times they were.

Listening to the two studio versions side-by-side, it's fair to say that there
are pros and cons for each. The original is an artefact of its time, and in
places, the 1970s engineering lets the music down, especially in passages
with wide dynamic range such as 'Dunkirk'. On the plus side, it sounds fresh
and has a naive simplicity in the arrangements.

With the 2013 version, the audio quality is an order of magnitude more
expansive, but in some places at the expense of the resultant pudding being
somewhat overegged, as with the cheesy and unnecessary pizzicato strings

in 'Sanctuary'. During the Radio Six interview in 2013, Latimer explains the rationale of the re-recording:

> I wanted to lovingly restore The Snow Goose, and so I wrote little vignettes so that the basic character is still the same and I've stayed true to a lot of different parts – even doing some of the same solos and things – but I just wanted it to be brought up to date. There's some different orchestrations and I think some of the passages are a real improvement.

In fact, in this writer's opinion, it's startlingly over-orchestrated, and in some places skirts on muzak: listen to the studio versions back-to-back, and you'll see. Also, with the re-recording, a few of the tracks have not just been re-recorded, but in today's parlance, 'reimagined' or rather *'revised'* as the album sleeve would have it. Nevertheless, as a way of getting the band playing again after Latimer's enforced absence, it serves its purpose well.

The live CD version is a gem, freshly cut and polished, then set in the form of the *A Live Record* expanded remaster.

That bit of necessary admin out of the way, back to the story. After the first two critically well-received but non-charting albums, the band elected to do a decidedly prog rock thing and create a concept album. Bardens came up with the first idea, based on Nobel Literature Prize-winner Herman Hesse's *Siddhartha*, which, although written in 1922, was by the 1970s regarded as a canonical new age tome that resonated with the end of the hippy era. One song on this theme was written with a single release in mind – Latimer's 'Riverman' – but this eventually ended up on the cutting room floor and the project was abandoned. Of course, some Camel fans will be familiar with the talented young British 21st-century Canterbury-revivalists, Syd Arthur – a direct reference to Hesse's *Meisterwerk*, so maybe Bardens was onto something after all.

Next up, Bardens suggested another Hesse novel, *Steppenwolf*, but this was also punted into the long grass as musically unworkable as well as being the name of the million-selling, but at that point defunct, 'Born To Be Wild' and eponymous Canadian-American hard rock tunesmiths. So the honour fell to Ferguson to suggest a work based on Paul Gallico's novella *The Snow Goose*. It was decided.

Honourably and sensibly, Camel did the right thing and approached the author for his blessing. However, Gallico took exception to the band using the name of the book and threatened to sue them for copyright infringement. The urban myth version of this situation is that the reason for Gallico's fit of pique was that (unsurprisingly, given the *Mirage* album cover) he associated the band with the cigarette brand and was a fervent anti-smoker. No doubt he had also been briefed on the shenanigans of the Camel cigarette marketing people during the recording of *Mirage* and subsequent tour.

Unsurprisingly, the truth is more prosaic: far from being anti-tobacco, Gallico was a lifelong pipe smoker, and although reportedly he vehemently objected to cigarettes – as many a militant pipe smoker is wont – the real reason for the dispute was that the rights to a musical association with the book had already been signed with songwriter Ed Welch, resulting in the schmaltzy and mostly forgotten 1976 orchestral oeuvre *The Snow Goose*, complete with a narration by none other than Chief Goon and WWII autobiographer, Spike Milligan. Whatever the reason, Camel's *Snow Goose* became *Music Inspired By The Snow Goose*, and litigation was side-stepped. The record managed to strike a chord beyond the British Isles and Camel achieved global, but most importantly, trans-Atlantic attention and a first worldwide hit.

Many critics at the time regarded the novella as overly sentimental, and its parallels with *The Hunchback of the Notre Dame* are there for all to see. But as the basis for an extended musical composition – with its wildly contrasting characters, bleak setting, WWII backdrop and, of course, a cute animal – it's perfect subject matter. I encourage all readers to give it a go – it will enhance your appreciation of the LP no end.

Written by Latimer and Bardens alone, album orchestrations were directed by David Bedford – who also conducted and arranged the LSO at the Royal Albert Hall gig later in the year (more on that to come). The individual LSO musicians were not credited on the LP, which is odd considering this was the heyday of the UK's Musicians Union.

A few rock bands had, in the previous few years, tried to do the 'live orchestra thing', most memorably with Deep Purple's *Concerto for Group & Orchestra* in 1969, and Rick Wakeman's *Journey to the Centre of the Earth* in 1974, with the former also at the Royal Albert Hall. Without at all wishing to disrespect Camel, it has to be recognised that both Purple and Wakeman, (through his association with Yes, who were then at the peak of their powers) were solid draws and already used to selling out stadiums and other premier venues, worldwide. In contrast, the largest venue that Camel had headlined thus far was The Roundhouse in London.

With the scene set, the gamble paid off and the growing commercial success of *Snow Goose* led to a sold-out performance in October 1975 at the Royal Albert Hall (this time not with a handful as in the studio, but with the full London Symphony Orchestra in tow), cementing the band's place in the ongoing annals of prog rock. If you believe what you read in multiple commentaries about that night, some members of the orchestra were less than chuffed about acting as a backing group for some bally pop musicians. Listening to the live document that comprises the second LP of the *A Live Record* double album, the classicists do sound somewhat listless at times. Not that the audience or reviewers cared: this gig is rightly counted amongst the landmark classics of the genre.

One final thing worth searching out is the appearance on *The Old Grey Whistle Test*, also in 1975 (included on the *Footage I* DVD): the band play with a small woodwind ensemble, and the 'chamber' setting is delightful.

Structurally, *Snow Goose* is akin to a classical tone poem, using leitmotifs in the manner of Wagner and Richard Strauss for the main characters – Rhayader, Fritha and, of course, the Snow Goose herself. These themes are punctuated by narrative sections – 'Rhayader Goes to Town', 'Sanctuary', 'Friendship', 'Dunkirk' and so on – carrying the story forward and subtly referencing the protagonists along the way. It all hangs together beautifully, and again we see that there is an extraordinary maturity to the composition. If you're familiar with the novella, then my notes on the story may seem redundant, but if you haven't read *The Snow Goose*, then I hope my references to the plot and characters will enhance your enjoyment of the music.

'The Great Marsh' (Latimer, Bardens)
Birdsong, calling geese, muted organ, celestial voices, waves splashing on the beach (beautifully realised by Andy Ward's soft-malleted cymbal work) – what more can you ask for as a prelude to Camel's most famous album? Anyone who's visited the Essex Marshes – where the book was set – or indeed any grey, desolate, shingly shoreline will instantly experience the illusion that this short passage evokes. When the band comes to the fore, backed by airy strings, in true overture style, we get a hint of what's to come – a lush, full sound that will continue throughout the piece. Get ready to soar.

'Rhayader' (Latimer, Bardens)
Immediately we're introduced to the main protagonist, the solitary, pained, disabled and disfigured artist living in an abandoned lighthouse: Rhayader. Latimer's flute motif – the 'Rhayader' Theme – is probably, outside of Camel fan circles, the most well-known of all the band's output. The counterpoint between flute and piano really is (and I'm not going to apologise for hyperbole) worthy of Bach or Mozart, and when the full band join in, it's wonderful to hear Ferguson's walking bass line brought forward in the mix while Latimer has fun with his wah-wah pedal. The organ solo is trademark Bardens, never overstepping the mark and sitting perfectly in the overall scene...

'Rhayader Goes To Town' (Latimer, Bardens)
...then, all at once, we're off to town, sprinting ahead at breakneck speed. The contrast between the shore and the town is cleverly made, and in the middle section, we're asked to imagine the conflict Rhayader feels by this change of location. He has to visit to procure supplies, his deformed figure being stared at by suspicious townsfolk, and there's no doubt where he'd rather be – it's masterfully evoked by Latimer's questioning guitar solo.

'Sanctuary' (Latimer, Bardens)
Rhayader is back at the lighthouse, staring at the ocean, palette in hand and brush poised above the canvas. His thoughts start to wander. This short and sweet interlude of lead guitar backed by fingerpicking acoustic paints a perfect little Impressionistic vignette before segueing into...

'Fritha' (Latimer, Bardens)

...Fritha's theme. At this stage, she's a young girl, maybe ten years old. The passage is written in E Minor, and that's a deliberate choice as one of this key's characteristics is regarded by musicologists as restlessness of spirit, perfect for a bedraggled, tousle-haired urchin, like Fritha. This image comes through in the melody and the nursery rhyme simplicity of this passage is another slice of compositional genius. Barden's Moog work over Latimer's acoustic is a 20th-century re-imagining of Baroque chamber music. Imagine a small pipe organ instead of the Moog and a lute instead of the guitar to get an inkling of where I'm going with this. 'Fritha', of course, just whets our appetite for what comes next, one of the most uplifting passages in rock music history.

'Snow Goose' (Latimer, Bardens)

Over a repeated single note 'ostinato' bass line, the legendary melody of the 'Snow Goose' theme melds with Echoplexed keyboard goose calls – a truly ground-breaking and imaginative solution to evoke the titular creature. As for 'The Great Marsh', the producer could easily have plopped in some tape of actual bird sounds, but this is so much better. The slow crescendo of the introduction surprisingly stops short of an implied and imminent climax, and we are treated to a guitar solo that can only be described as elixir of Latimer, an alchemist's sublimation of everything that, in my opinion, makes the guitarist the most emotive and melodic of all his contemporaries – Gilmour, Hackett, Hillage and Howe included. His touch is so light, yet so intense, so precise, bending the strings only enough and only when absolutely necessary – not as an axeman's showy, superfluous technical flourish. When Latimer plays, you can see him become one with the instrument. It's transcendental.

'Friendship' (Latimer, Bardens)

Fritha sees that the bird is injured – by gunshot – and separated from her flock, so takes her to Rhayader. This is a critical element of the narrative: as geese mate with the same partner for life, the 'friendship' of the title is on multiple planes. Two are new, and the other long-standing, thereby layering the pathos perfectly as the Snow Goose is injured both physically and emotionally. Now, instead of Moog, bassoon and oboe take the role of the singular goose. It's easy to picture her waddling around Fritha and Rhayader – her webbed feet the bassoon, and talking to the humans with upturned head and a questioning angle to her neck – the oboe. This is wonderful, magical in its execution. Again, for this passage, the classically based counterpoint is exemplary, which is why the almost 180° shift in tempo and style of the next section works so well.

'Migration' (Latimer, Bardens)

Drum roll, please ... literally. Those of a certain age might well remember the vocal accompaniment to the 1970s Pearl & Dean cinema adverts and the 'da-da-da-da' voices on 'Migration' do veer worryingly in that direction. Additionally, the incessant Hammond 'quacks' are a little cheesy given the avian context. On the plus side, the almost 160 beats per minute rhythm does elicit visions of birds flying fast and high, so in the end, 'Migration' works as an interlude, especially as it slows down at the finish implying the end of a journey. All in all, though, not Snow Goose's finest 1/30th of an hour.

'Rhayader Alone' (Latimer, Bardens)
The 'Rhayader' theme is reprised, this time on electric piano interwoven with ethereal lead guitar. Rhayader has lost touch with Fritha as well as the snow goose. The piece evokes the atmosphere of solitude really well, as the protagonist ponders his life and situation and, it is to be supposed, his growing fondness for Fritha – unseen by him, but now presumably a young woman.

'Flight Of The Snow Goose' (Latimer, Bardens)
Overlapping arpeggiations on synths build gradually, inferring that something is approaching. In the context of the story, this acts as an interlude describing the to-ing and fro-ing of the snow goose on its annual migrations. The runs up and down the scales from all instruments with subtle changes in tempo and dynamics, perfectly capture the image of soaring flight.

'Preparation' (Latimer, Bardens)
Woodwind takes centre stage with a duet between flute and oboe, then synth and guitar over a wordless and slightly spooky vocal track, together suggesting danger on the horizon. Rhayader is packing supplies into his boat while Fritha watches and asks where he is going. He tells her about the troops surrounded in Dunkirk, 100 miles away by sea and how he is going to participate in the 'little ships' rescue flotilla. Fritha pleads with him not to go, but when Rhayader uses an analogy of the soldiers trapped on the beach being like a flock of hunted birds – just like the ones they had been rescuing and tending during the years of their friendship – she relents, but not after pleading to join him. Rhayader refuses to let her board.

'Dunkirk' (Latimer, Bardens)
'Dunkirk' is the longest single track on the record, and the switching of the first section between 4/4 and 5/4 time is a cunning way to represent the marching of soldiers interspersed with them ducking for cover under gun and mortar fire. Bass and organ are soon joined by lead guitar playing a mournful melody that suggests chaos and confusion, then occasional blasts of orchestral horns add to the martial atmosphere.

Building to a climax, with marching-band drum rolls becoming a feature, at the three-and-a-half-minute mark, there's a change of mood and tempo, signifying the final frantic ferrying of the combatants from the beach to the waiting ships under incessant gunfire. Latimer's soloing here brilliantly captures the mood and climaxes in a discordant finale that borrows from the 'Mars' movement in Holst's 'Planet Suite'. Ward's gong splash brings the passage to an appropriately epic close.

Summing up, 'Dunkirk' is a vivid musical evocation of the evacuation, during which Rhayader saves many lives by countless hours of moving soldiers between the beach and a hospital ship, the 'Kentish Maid' (in real life, the SS Maid Of Kent which was indeed present at Dunkirk).

'Epitaph' (Latimer, Bardens)

'Epitaph' starts with the same theme as 'Dunkirk'. Processed percussion including tubular bells recalling Britten's 'War Requiem' – the passage gradually fading out. Rhayader is dead in his boat; he has been machine-gunned. The Snow Goose is with him, grieving, warning any other ship that comes close to stay away. Eventually, the Snow Goose flies away, and the boat sinks. On a lighter note, *Mirage* had a can of beer; *Snow Goose* got Ferguson's duffle coat, which you can just about hear, deep in the mix, around the 30-second mark and supposedly representing the flapping of wings. No one can argue that Camel weren't at the cutting edge of mid-70s sound effects.

'Fritha Alone' (Latimer, Bardens)

'Fritha Alone' is a variation on the 'Fritha' theme, this time in A Minor, played magnificently by Bardens solo at the grand piano. This key suggests womanhood, maturity, and at the same time, a certain melancholy, so again we see how Latimer and Bardens have used classical theory to underpin their writing.

'La Princesse Perdue' (Latimer, Bardens)

Early in the book, Rhayader names the Snow Goose 'La Princesse Perdue', but here the name garners a double meaning. Not only is the snow goose now truly lost forever, but Fritha is also a lost princess – lost in her thoughts of unrequited love for Rhayader. Now in a major key, the music evokes happy memories, although these interspersed with sadness and regret by modulations into the minor – suitably upbeat on the one hand and yet melancholy on the other, and reminiscent in places of Wakeman's early solo work. Backed by a soaring string arrangement, the music includes multiple references to the various themes and motifs earlier in the work, a reprise in the fullest sense of the word.

'The Great Marsh' (reprise) (Latimer, Bardens)

And so, we end as we began, on the Great Marsh. Bird calls; ethereal backing voices; simple alternating electric piano chords; Ward using mallets on the cymbals to evoke waves splashing on the shore; all gradually fading to black. We've reached the end; what a wonderful, emotional and inspirational journey it has been.

Moonmadness (1976)

Personnel:
Andrew Latimer: guitar, vocals
Peter Bardens: keyboards, vocals
Doug Ferguson: bass, vocals
Andy Ward: drums, percussion
Produced at Basing Street Studios, London, January / February 1976 by Rhett Davies
Release date: 26 March 1976.
Running time: 39:15
Current edition: Decca 8829312
Highest Chart Places: 15 (UK), USA (118)

Now cemented as the 'classic' line-up, by 1976, Camel were a global brand, and Deram was drooling at the prospect of 'Son Of Snow Goose' and maybe a couple of Top Ten hits to go with it – an irksomely recurring theme as we will discover as the story unfolds. But thankfully, and with minimal interference from the label during the recording sessions, the band stubbornly ploughed ahead on their own terms and delivered a work of art that many – fans and musos alike – regard as the band's masterpiece: *Moonmadness*. Bearing this out, the critics at the time were fulsome in their praise. Said Lisa Eliscu of *Phonograph Record* magazine in 1976:

> The music is restrained, wistful, pretty … in the face of disco, and with its Latin rhythms, jazz fusion influences, Camel has made an album of dreams and clouds.

Reviewing the band's 1976 Fairfield Halls, Croydon performance on the *Moonmadness* Tour, Chris Welch of *Melody Maker*, not exactly renowned for hyperbole, effused:

> Camel have broken through into that undefinable sunlit area where a group becomes a supergroup.

Finally, also reviewing the Croydon gig, John Tobler of soon-to-be punk and new-wave bible *New Musical Express*, stated:

> [Camel are] a band to reckon with … Andy Latimer will be a guitar hero ranking with Clapton, Beck and Page.

The esteem in which *Moonmadness* is held continues to recent times, and it's frankly impossible for me to improve on what Mikael Åkerfeldt of Opeth said in an interview with *Guitar World in* 2014:

> I was already in my twenties when I first heard it. I was working at a record store in Stockholm at the time, and one of my co-workers, who was in his early

forties, suggested I check out Camel. I bought a couple of their albums on second-hand vinyl, including Moonmadness and The Snow Goose, and took them home on a lunch break. I was floored by Moonmadness and especially by Andy Latimer's guitar playing. It was just what I'd been looking for — finally, someone to copy! I had always leaned toward hard-rock players like Richie Blackmore, but this was something new. It was so heartfelt and emotional, and every note felt like it served a purpose. I was also amazed by the compositions, as well as the solos, and of course, Latimer's guitar tone. One of the best guitar solos is in a song called 'Lunar Sea.' It's long and fantastically executed. He really builds it to a splendid climax. It's as perfect as an album gets – plays like a classical tone poem, with every note in the right place and the track ordering supreme.

Given the above, there's no question that Camel created something rather special during those three weeks in Notting Hill spanning January and February 1976.

Moonmadness had its gestation when Latimer and Bardens spent a bucolic few weeks at a farmhouse in the southeast of England's 'stockbroker belt'. Speaking to Pete Jones on the *Tales From The Tiger Moth* podcast in 2016, Latimer recalls:

Pete and I, we camped out in this farm near Dorking and that was kind of what instigated the title in a way because Pete and I were both convinced that the house we were living in was haunted. Pete especially tuned into the spirit of things. His father wrote lots of books on the occult and spirits, so he talked about it, and we were saying one night 'it gets kind of mad when there is a full moon'. And I sort of, just to be funny, said 'we're going to get some sort of moonmadness'. It kind of stuck.

As a framework for the LP, Latimer and Bardens came up with the idea of writing a song for each member of the band; songs that would reflect the characters and personalities of the musicians. So it was that four numbers emerged following that plan: 'Chord Change' for Bardens, 'Another Night' for Ferguson, 'Air Born' for Latimer and, presciently given what was to come, 'Lunar Sea' for Ward.

Following the purely instrumental *Snow Goose, Moonmadness* marked a return to vocal tracks and four of the seven pieces have lyrical content. Despite the aforementioned criticism of their vocal abilities, the band stuck to their guns by not hiring a dedicated singer; a lasting effect of deciding to carry on with their own vocals was that the band kept them low in the mix and used effects including the revolving Leslie horn speaker (the peripheral to the inimitable Hammond B3 responsible for its trademark wobbly sound), phasing, chorusing and echo to conceal them – albeit in plain sight – in the mix. It may have been coyness on their parts, but in the end, serendipitously, this vocal processing only added to the unique Camel sound.

Latimer is on record saying that he felt the *Moonmadness* recording process was rushed, and indeed just three weeks to commit to tape a work as monumental as *Moonmadness* does on reflection seem a tad too hasty considering bands like Yes (with *Tales*) and Floyd (with *Wish You Were Here*) were during that period spending months in the studio to deliver the finished product. Admittedly, Yes and Floyd had much bigger sellers under their belts, and thus presumably bigger budgets to work with, but nevertheless, Latimer's point is well made. Happily, though, you would never know from *Moonmadness* as, to paraphrase Åkerfeldt, it really is as damn near perfect as two sides of vinyl gets. Now, onto the music.

'Aristillus' (Latimer)

Although credited to Latimer alone, 'Aristillus' was written as a result of jamming between Bardens and Latimer in their rural retreat, but they had no idea what to call it. As the rest of the band already knew the title of the album, Andy Ward had been doing some background reading on all things moon-related. On hearing the drumless track, he started repeating the words 'Aristillus, Autolycus' to the music, usually followed by fits of the giggles, and then explained that he had been reading about the moon and all the fantastic names there were for the craters. Aristillus stuck, and if you listen closely to the end of the cut, you'll hear Mr Ward doing his thing, this time without corpse-ing. This was the first as well as the last time his vocals appear on a Camel track.

It's the perfect entry point to the album, not too long, not too short, and a tasty amuse-bouche for the six courses of delights to come. As a concert opener, it works outstandingly.

'Song Within A Song' (Latimer, Bardens)

Don't go looking for any meaning in the song title because, according to Latimer, there isn't any – it just seemed like a great name for the piece. As for the lyrics, in conversation with Peter Jones, Latimer recounted:

> Pete loved words, so sometimes he'd write a lyric and it wouldn't mean much, but it would sound nice. So, the song isn't about much, really.

From my perspective, I think that Edgar Allan Poe's 'Dream Within A Dream' must have been a subliminal inspiration, as the first part of the song most certainly has a dreamlike quality, with soft waves of sound and an almost lullaby-like lilt. Latimer's tender flute playing sets the scene with the band very much in the background, followed by two short verses, interspersed with more lovely flute, and Ferguson on vocal duty. Choosing Ferguson over himself or Bardens for this track prompted Latimer to observe, again when chatting with Peter Jones:

> Doug sung that number, which was strange because it has a choirboy feel to it, but he's a big, beefy sergeant major!

Nonetheless, Doug's relaxed tones fit the song like a glove, so ultimately, strange or otherwise, I think the guys made the right choice here.

After those vocals, we really get into the meat of the track with an instrumental bridge that leads into one of the classic Camel passages – Bardens' canonical melodic Moog solo, beloved of many an 'air keyboard' player ('Guilty as charged, yer honour'). Lasting over a minute, with the band driving him along at a brisk pace, we can see that over the previous few years, Bardens had progressed from a purely Hammond virtuoso to a keyboard player that was right at home with synths as well. Sure, he wasn't as technically brilliant or flashy as, say, Keith Emerson, but I'd argue that his restraint makes his contribution all the more fitting for the finished product. Anyway, it's a terrific solo and perfectly prefaces the epic final section of the number. Latimer reminisced with Jones in 2016:

> Pete and I were always a great partnership – we worked really well as a writing partnership. If either of us had the inspiration for the music, the other one would just sit back and let them go with it. Pete and I always seemed to be on the same wavelength – he would be happy to just play it again. So 'Song Within A Song' was very much a 50:50 relationship. He was always very quirky, and I was simple and melodic, so that song just worked.

Yes, indeed – work it does, and typical of Camel yet again, we've witnessed just so much content in so short a time – another four-movement mini-symphony. 'Song Within in a Song' remains a fixture in the live sets and sits firmly in my top ten. I'm in good company, as Latimer counts it as one of his favourite pieces too. And we're only two tracks into the LP.

'Chord Change' (Latimer, Bardens)

Now we get to the first of the 'portrait' pieces. Bardens was seen by Latimer as very changeable, inasmuch as he changed moods very quickly. At the same time, Bardens had a reputation as a very laid back, humorous chap, but with that came the occasional drama too. Hence 'Chord Change'. As co-written with Latimer, it's clear that Bardens wasn't offended by the characterisation and it's plain to see that, in fact, he went 'all in' when it comes to the keyboard parts.

'Chord Change' kicks off at a mighty gallop, chorused guitar to the fore and keys held back, with the rhythm section fairly kicking the proverbial. The second section really swings, with Ward at one point making fun and economical use of a Vibraslap before focusing on Latimer with another of his restrained, melodic and frankly perfect, extended solos – backed subtly on organ and marred only by more of those 'da da, da da' backing vocals just before the soloing starts.

Next up, we have a masterclass in Hammond from Bardens – a craftsman-constructed tour-de-force that soon encompasses Moog as well, segueing into the double-time endpiece again driven along by Ward's jazzy inflexions

– especially with snare and hi-hat, and Ferguson's fine walking bass lines. It's a shame that on the studio version, the number fades out, as when compared with the live performances, we miss out on an expected climax. It seems like an odd decision by the producer, but one with which we have to live.

'Spirit Of The Water' (Bardens)

After the acrobatics of 'Chord Change', 'Spirit of the Water' is a welcome change of pace, as well as – in a live setting – giving the drummer a chance to catch his breath for a couple of minutes. Bardens' heavily processed vocals float over an Eric Satie-esque piano melody, and the song literally flows along from beginning to end, with Latimer joining on recorder for the middle section. 'Pete said, look, I got this idea and he played me the whole piece and I said, 'wow, this is fantastic, we don't need to do any overdubs. We can just add a recorder'. He wrote the lyrics but did not have a title: I was reading a book called *Salar The Salmon* by Henry Williamson (he of *Tarka the Otter* fame) and one of the last lines in that book is something about the spirit of the water'. There you have it.

'Another Night' (Latimer, Bardens, Ward, Ferguson)

Remember what Mikael Åkerfeldt said about track ordering? At this stage in our listen, we're starting to understand what he was driving at. The pretty interlude of 'Spirit of the Water' gives nothing away in anticipation of 'Another Night', the second of the album's character studies, this time of the bassist. Latimer: 'He [Doug] was extremely forthright and always getting into crazy escapades', and the lyrics certainly infer that Ferguson had been on a boozy bender-or-three during his time with the band.

A crescendo-ing keyboard and lead guitar intro, highly reminiscent, possibly deliberately, of the opening to 'Lady Fantasy', gets us going on this, the band's bluesiest track since 'Separation' on *Camel*. 'Another Night' fairly drives ahead on an unreconstructed double-time 6/4 beat, pausing only momentarily towards the end for another of Latimer's Hillage-influenced glissando breaks before we're back to the thumping backbeat of the opening, supporting a few bars of classic Hammond work from Bardens. Considering Ward's famously light touch and precision behind the kit, for once, hearing him beating the merry hell out of the skins is great to witness.

In an album of classics, though, and despite its release as a cut-down single version, 'Another Night' is the least memorable of the seven. It seems to me to be missing that proverbial *je ne sais quoi* that all the others have, but naturally, that's just my opinion and I'm sure some readers will have this down as one of their faves.

The B-side of the single was a live recording of 'Lunar Sea' from Hammersmith Odeon in 1976. Due to its ten-minute length and appearance on a 7" record, this has the odd distinction of being 33 1/3 rpm and not the usual 45 rpm of the A-side. Gimmick? Maybe, but it served its purpose in introducing listeners to one of Camel's longer-form numbers. Bear in mind also that this is not the version that was to appear on *A Live Record*, which came from a gig at Bristol's Colston Hall on the *Rain Dances* tour in 1977, but it is on the 2002 remaster of *Moonmadness* as bonus content.

'Air Born' (Latimer, Bardens)

'Air Born' is the prettiest song on the record. If the 'character' songs were allied to 'The Four Seasons', this would undoubtedly be summer. All the band saw Latimer as the most quintessentially English member of the group, which according to Latimer in 2016 on *Tales From The Tiger Moth*, apparently presented a challenge to him when working on the number:

> When I was writing 'Air Born', I had to discard all the American influence that I'd had from my youth, so I was trying to be very English and be myself – so I saw myself as this guy who lived in the forest, which was a bit bizarre.

Flute and piano in a style nothing less than a contemporary interpretation of classical chamber music act as an atmospheric preface for what is to come: the chemistry that Latimer and Bardens had at this time is plain for all to see, and immediately we're transported to the hedgerows, spinneys, rolling hills and patchwork fields of Middle England. Just as we're being lulled into this agrarian vibe, in typical Camel fashion, there's a complete shift in instrumentation with Latimer's guitar soaring over Barden's string synth (for those keyboard geeks among us, the recently introduced Roland RS-202 Strings, which is also a feature on 'Lunar Sea') and perfectly judged drum fills from Ward.

'Air Born' is a prime example of Latimer's vocals processed through the Leslie speaker, and this treatment suits the mood of the song extremely well – an instance of more is, for once, actually more from a production perspective.

After a couple of sung verses, the music takes a folky turn with flute overlaid on fingerstyle acoustic guitar before featuring an unusual guitar sound over electric piano. Of this for want of a better word, 'floaty' guitar solo, Latimer recalls that he and co-producer Rhett Davies spent a whole afternoon plugging guitars into Moogs, fuzz boxes and all sorts of equipment to get the sound they were looking for: 'When we listened to the result we thought 'this just sounds like a bad keyboard!'"… but bad keyboard or not, it remained on the tape and sounds just great in the context of the song as a whole. So, I may be stretching an analogy here, but if 'Air Born' can be regarded as a Bachian prelude, then what comes next is most certainly the fugue.

'Lunar Sea' (Latimer, Bardens)

In my 'Aristillus' critique at the start of this section, I wrote that I see *Moonmadness* as akin to a gourmet seven-course tasting menu, so now we reach the grand finale, a dessert course straight out of some 18th-century French palace cookbook. It is a banquet table, Carême-created centrepiece construction of intricate detail yet monumental dimensions: quite literally *La Piece de Resistance:* 'Lunar Sea', Camel's prog-fusion masterpiece.

String synths, gliss guitar, bass pedals, wind chimes, mallets splashing on cymbals and Andy Ward blowing bubbles through a rubber hose into a bucket of water. This is another push of the SFX envelope by our fantastic four. The whole effect of this intro is bloody brilliant and, for me as a tender thirteen-year-old, was revelatory. Live renditions are even more epic, with the overlay of the Apollo XI radio feed – it's a real missed opportunity that this wasn't thought of in the studio, but I'm nit-picking here.

After the intro, we get into the meat of the number, and what a treat for the ears it is: the whole band giving it their all, keys and guitar in perfect synch, powered by that jazzy Ferguson bassline and Ward's swinging drums – listen to the hi-hat and cymbal work, it's incredible. Just as we're getting settled into that urgent 5/4 tempo, they do it again – a change of pace and *that* utterly fabulous Moog solo, to a pure jazz-funk backdrop from the rhythm section, with a few clever licks from Latimer punctuating the synths.

Then the wig out: Camel had recently been on tour supporting Soft Machine, who at that point in their evolution had revered guitar god Allan Holdsworth on six-string. According to the *musicaficianado* blog in 2018, Latimer has stated:

We were impressed by Soft Machine, and Allan Holdsworth was the guitar player. Andy [Ward] and I sat at the side of the stage every night with our mouths open. We got hang up on jazz. Pete came up with that corky riff. I wrote that end riff, which is really quite Soft Machine.

There's no arguing with that because the band come together magnificently, led by a guitar solo worthy of the greatest. The solo should quieten any naysayers regarding Latimer's chops – on this showing, he plainly has them to spare but has spent his career using them sparingly. Style-wise, he's more of a threader than a shredder, and Camel's output wouldn't be the same without his calculated approach.

'Lunar Sea' comes to its end with a trademark Camel reprise of the opening, but now in double-time, followed by, of course, the thunder – created in the studio using an unwieldy metal 'Thunder Sheet', and on the original vinyl with an infinite scroll groove meaning that the record – and so the thunder – would keep playing until the needle was manually lifted off.

'Lunar Sea' hasn't dated a millisecond since it was first committed to tape and what an album closer. It is music of the highest quality and way ahead of its time. However you listen to 'Lunar Sea', headphones or speakers, in the car or in the garden, this track needs to be played loud. And often.

This marks the end of an era for Camel, stylistically, as the band were about to move into a more fusion-based direction and structurally as this was the last time we'd hear Ferguson on the four-string: the story continues with *Rain Dances.*

Associated Tracks
Both of these tracks are available only on the *Moondances* DVD that was released by Camel Productions in 2007. They were recorded during the *Moonmadness* sessions but never made it to vinyl.

'Autumn' (Latimer)
A pleasant little ditty, but it's not difficult to see why it didn't make the cut. What is remarkable, though, are Ferguson's vocals which are, like on 'Song Within A Song', just lovely – a completely under-rated vocalist. Lyric-wise, Autumn is rather 'schoolboy poetry' in substance and the track is saved by an extended, very American-sounding solo from Latimer.

'Riverman' (Latimer)
This is another vocal track, this time with Latimer as the singer. I suspect this one was also inspired by Williamson's *Salar The Salmon* mentioned in the 'Spirit of the Water section', and as with 'Autumn', it's unsurprising that it wasn't committed to vinyl. Nevertheless, these two historical artefacts remain interesting in their own right, and it's good to have them out there.

Rain Dances (1977)

Personnel:
Andrew Latimer: guitar, vocals
Peter Bardens: keyboards, vocals
Richard Sinclair: bass, vocals
Andy Ward: drums, percussion
Mel Collins: Soprano sax, alto sax, tenor sax, clarinet, bass clarinet, bass flute, concert flute
Additional musicians:
Martin Drover: trumpet on 'One of These Days I'll Get an Early Night', flugelhorn on 'Skylines'
Malcolm Griffiths: trombone on 'One of These Days I'll Get an Early Night' and 'Skylines'
Brian Eno: Minimoog, electric piano, piano on 'Elke'
Fiona Hibbert: harp on 'Elke'
Produced at Basing Street Studios, London, February-August 1977 by Rhett Davies and Camel
Release date: 17 September 1977.
Running time: 41:10
Current edition: Decca CD 531 4610
Highest chart places: UK:20, USA:136

By the *Rain Dances* sessions, it was becoming plain to the other members that Ward was getting itchy feet about the type of music they had produced to date. In those halcyon mid-70s days, they were listening to lots of different bands, like the aforementioned Soft Machine as well as Brand X, Weather Report, Return to Forever and a lot of the other jazz-rock fusion material that was in vogue around that time. Latimer recounted to Peter Jones in 2016:

> I think Andy was getting to a point where he said to Pete [Bardens] and I 'You know, look, either we've got to replace Doug, or I'm going to leave' and it was such a difficult period because we had a chemistry as four people, and everybody had a role.

It's worth hearing in its entirety what Latimer has to say about the time, as the following passage, from 2016 in conversation with Pete Jones on his Podcast *Tales From The Tiger Moth*, gets to the root of the horrible challenges he, in particular, was facing, in no small degree due to Ferguson being the first 'hire' of the classic line-up, as well as Doug introducing Ward to the group:

> I could see Andy (W)'s point of view and I was writing tough bass lines – I wrote 'Skylines' for Andy, and the bass line is something I ended up playing on the album. It was incredibly difficult – it took three takes – I couldn't play it all the way through, so I realised that after I'd written the piece that Doug

wouldn't be able to play it. Then Pete came up with an idea for 'Tell Me' and I'd written a fretless bass part that I also knew that he wouldn't be able to play, which I ended up again playing on the album, but we were both – Pete and I – thinking 'Oh goodness – Doug's not going to be able to play fretless, he's not going to be able to play 'Skylines', and we're going to lose our drummer if we keep Doug'. So we went with Andy – and in the end, on reflection, I think it was a bad decision. I should have just played it on the record and we should have just worked around it. The whole dynamics of the band changed when Doug left.

Now bass-less, apart from Latimer's decision to step in on the two fretless tracks, for the first time in just short of a decade, the search was on for a four-string man. You might be puzzled as to why Camel then chose a jobbing carpenter and kitchen fitter to fill the role, until the penny drops that said *joiner* was Richard Sinclair, in semi-retirement after the dissolution of Hatfield & The North in 1975. Sinclair, a founder member of Caravan, was almost too obvious a choice given the overlap in style and philosophy between the two bands, but chosen indeed he was – and not just for his bass playing: his vocal talents suited the Camel sound too. Sinclair fondly recalls his time with the band, as evidenced by his comments in an interview with *HitChannel.com* in 2016:

I think that was a special time for me. When I joined the band, the music for Rain Dances was ready, so I just recorded it. I went there and I really enjoyed what I did. I think my playing was a bit more reserved doing Camel music because it was structured in a certain way. Camel was the most professional band I have ever been in.

Almost inevitably, perhaps, this collaboration prompted some of the jokers in the press pack to dub the new line-up as 'Caramel' – catchier than 'Yuggles' for sure, but thankfully it didn't stick.

Cementing the fusion direction of the band, *Rain Dances* marked the beginning of the band's four-year association with ex-King Crimson and in-demand session man Mel Collins on sax and woodwind.

Released on 17 September 1977, just one day after Marc Bolan was killed in a car crash that dominated the music press for weeks, *Rain Dances* would be the last LP the band recorded at Basing Street as well as the last with Rhett Davies at the helm. It was also the longest time that Camel had spent in the studio on an album as recording, on and off, spanned seven months from February to August 1977 – a reflection of the hunt for the new bassist.

One final observation is that Bardens has no vocal credits on *Rain Dances*, which is odd. Rumours continue to this day that this was due to Sinclair effectively making Bardens' role as a singer redundant and is one of the first indications of the tension that would boil over between the two during the sessions for *Breathless* the following year.

'First Light' (Latimer, Bardens)

As uplifting an album opener as you could wish for and giving more than a cursory, appreciative nod back in the direction of 'Lunar Sea'. Sinclair's jazz-inflected bass lines immediately raise their metaphorical heads in the mix without overwhelming the overall effect, and we also get our first taste of saxophone in the shape of Mel Collins' outro. Smiles all round, then, and any fears fans may have had that the departure of Ferguson would result in a dramatic change of direction seem to have been put to bed.

'Metrognome' (Latimer, Bardens)

We've already seen that Camel have a knack of combining mini 'movements' into a cohesive whole – for example, 'Freefall' and 'Song Within A Song' – and in 'Metrognome', this approach again pays huge dividends for listeners. What starts as Ward's clever tick-tocking on woodblocks (the eponymous metronome), vocals and instruments in unison slice of whimsy, with just a hint of a chorus, at the two-minute mark the song segues into a jazzy mid-section with the sax prominently featured to start with, followed by an intricate Latimer solo. Then, just when you're settling into that groove, off we go on a minute-and-change prog rock blowout of Valhallan proportions, centring on an epic guitar solo. And all this in the space of four minutes. Stirring stuff.

'Tell Me' (Latimer, Bardens)

If Camel put out a compilation album of ballads from the Bardens era, it's likely fans would feel a tad short-changed, but one of the few tracks on such a collection would be 'Tell Me'. In a nutshell, it's a pretty and on the surface inconsequential helping of schmalz, saved in large part by Latimer on fretless bass and, to its credit, certainly different to anything that went before.

'Highways To The Sun' (Latimer, Bardens)

This is a real pop-prog stomper in a syncopated march time, with Latimer at the upper reaches of his vocal range and on occasion sounding somewhat out of breath. The single version – erroneously called 'Highways Of The Sun' on the remaster – is chopped down by a pretty much invisible 30 seconds. Both versions are so singalong-able and filled with catchy riffs that this could well have been the elusive hit that Decca so desperately wanted – if it had been released two years earlier. The UK pop scene during the Autumn of 1977 wasn't exactly fertile ground for this sort of thing, so it didn't chart; *Never Mind The Bollocks* hit the shelves a mere six weeks after *Rain Dances* was released. Those were the days …

'Unevensong' (Latimer, Bardens, Ward)

And now we reach the first, real, Camel classic on *Rain Dances*, and it's been worth the wait. Opening Side Two of the LP, it's a guaranteed shoo-in for any live set, and in the space of a mere five-and-a-half minutes, 'Unevensong' is the band presented in a hand-crafted crystal decanter, bottled at cask strength and non-chill filtered. All the hallmarks of the Bardens era are present and correct: tremendous tightness and musicianship, multi-section, multi-tempo, multi-key, with heavily-processed vocals and all building up to a joyous climax.

'Unevensong' is a double pun, as this jaunty and upbeat song is both uneven in meter, structure and key. It's also about as far away from a choral evensong as you can get: dashed cunning, those Camel boys.

Kicking off in Supertramp-like style with an electric piano riff underpinned by some cracking bass playing and drumming, two verses of vocal harmonies – in this guise, pretty much a first for the band and led by Sinclair – come in early, flowing into the slower second movement of squealing guitar and meaty left-hand notes on Moog that melds into a trademark Bardens synth solo. Then imperceptibly, the tempo picks up and we're back to the first theme, but only for three bars which modulate from major to minor, a lilting third, full-band motif develops together with a vocal bridge, then we're gathering pace and back to a variation on the original melody for the final minute-or-so. Exceptional.

If you're allowed only one track that might convince a Camel non-believer to have an epiphany, this is probably it.

'One of These Days I'll Get An Early Night' (Latimer, Bardens, Ward, Sinclair, Collins)

Camel's instrumental jazz-rock talents get full rein with 'One of These Days ...', which can be considered as a studio companion piece to 'Liggin' at Louis'' live-only effort. The influences are obvious: Chick Corea, Weather Report or Colosseum could all have recorded this, plopped it on an LP, and nobody would have been the wiser. But don't take this as a criticism; it's intended as praise of the highest order: while the aforementioned giants of the genre raked in the Gold Records and associated cash, Camel stayed bubbling under with their audience of mainly prog aficionados. Double-tracked saxes, chorused and echoplexed guitar, funky Fender Rhodes piano and an unremitting groove – this is mid-Seventies jazz rock par excellence: the cream on the fusion cake is Latimer's closing solo, so patently and abundantly influenced by Holdsworth.

As an aside at this point, I often wonder if maybe it's because Camel were so early on labelled as progressive rock that the band flew under the radar of the more mainstream fusion fans. One can only speculate as to how successful they would have been sales-wise if they'd come to the attention of that audience: after all, Latimer, in many interviews, has come back to the theme that 'we were predominantly an instrumental band'. I've put all the fusion-y tracks together in a playlist at the end of this book, together with a suggestion for the 'powers that be': I'm convinced such a collection would bring Camel a new and lucrative audience even now in the 21st Century.

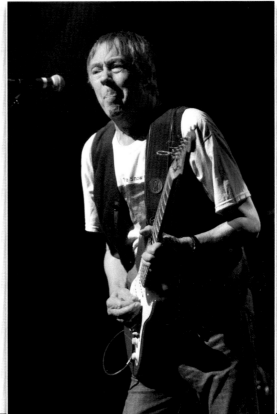

Right: Latimer and 'that red guitar' on the 'Retirement Sucks' tour at The Paradiso in Amsterdam in 2013. (*Bert Treep*)

Below: The inimitable Mr Bass in all his hirsute glory, and still playing one of his favoured Wal basses, on stage at *Night of the Prog* at The Loreley in 2018. (*Bert Treep*)

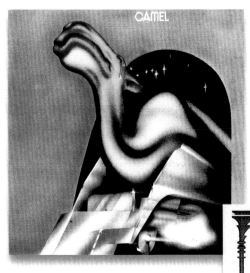

Left: The less-than-successful debut album – commercially at least – from 1973. (*MCA*)

Below: The band's first classic – *Mirage*, released in 1974. (*Decca*)

Above: The original and somewhat fanciful US cover for *Mirage*, released in 1974.

Right: The album that gave the band its first real commercial success, *Music Inspired By The Snow Goose*, released in 1975. (*Decca*)

Right: *Moonmadness* (1976). Another hit in the UK, the album saw the band's profile increase in Europe and the USA. (*Decca*)

Below: A somewhat different take on the idea of *Moonmadness* for the US cover in 1976.

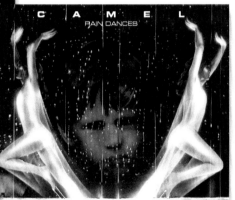

Above: *Rain Dances* (1977). The first lineup change saw Doug Ferguson replaced by Richard Sinclair and heralded a slightly jazzier new direction. (*Decca*)

Left: *Breathless* (1978) saw the partnership of Peter Bardens and Andrew Latimer splinter. It was never to be repaired – professionally at least. (*Decca*)

CAMEL   Andy Latimer   GEMINI

GEMINI

Andy Ward

CAMEL

This page: Andrew Latimer and Andy Ward from a full set of promotional cards from around 1975 of the original band members, very much in the style of the time. (*Private collection of Shane Carlson*)

This page: Peter Bardens and Doug Ferguson
complete the full set of promotional cards.
(*Private collection of Shane Carlson*)

Greasy Truckers live at Dingwalls Dancehall
Featuring Camel, Henry Cow, Gong &
Global Village Trucking Company
Double Album Set £2.00

Left: A newspaper advert for the legendary *Greasy Truckers* double album in 1973. Why the label chose to use an image of an un-named 60s-era beat combo is anyone's guess. (*Private collection of Shane Carlson*)

Right and below: The notorious promotional 'free pack of five' given away during the *Mirage* tour, otherwise known as 'The Jukes Boxes'. (*Private collection of Shane Carlson*)

Right: A Flyer for the 21 February 1981 concert on the *Nude* tour at Friar's, Aylesbury, England. (*Private collection of Shane Carlson*)

Left: A pristine example of one of only a handful of surviving posters for the landmark Royal Albert Hall performance of *The Snow Goose* in October 1975. (*Private collection of Shane Carlson*)

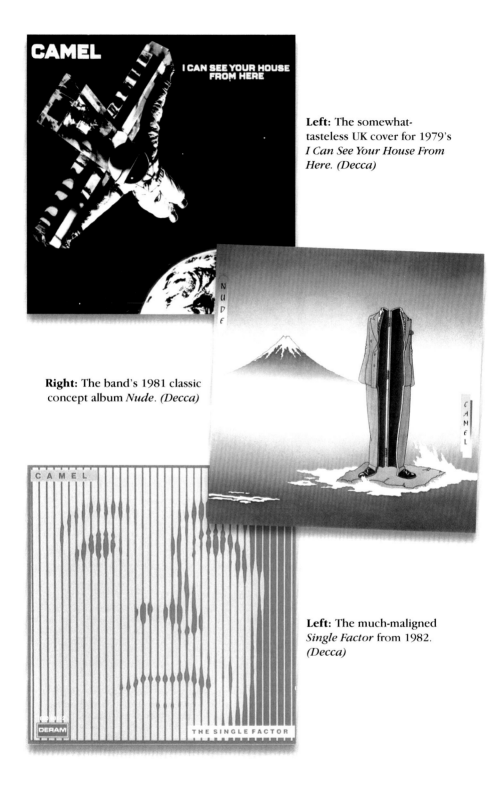

Left: The somewhat-tasteless UK cover for 1979's *I Can See Your House From Here*. (Decca)

Right: The band's 1981 classic concept album *Nude*. (Decca)

Left: The much-maligned *Single Factor* from 1982. (Decca)

Right: The last album of the 1980s, *Stationary Traveller*. It was to be the last album for Decca, and also the last before an extended hiatus which saw Latimer and partner Susan Hoover relocate to the USA. (*Decca*)

Left: After a break of seven years, Camel returned with *Dust And Dreams* on their own label – based on John Steinbeck's *The Grapes Of Wrath*, in 1991. (*Camel Productions*)

Right: The band's next album was *Harbour Of Tears*, released in 1996, inspired by the site of many emigrations from Ireland to the USA. (*Camel Productions*)

Left: We thought it would never happen again: Colin Bass and Jason Hart back on stage after Latimer's illness, at the Paradiso in Amsterdam on the 'Retirement Sucks' / re-recorded Snow Goose tour in 2013. (*Bert Treep*)

Right: Guy LeBlanc at the Paradiso in 2013: 'One of the greatest joys of my life was the opportunity to join Camel for the 'Retirement Sucks' tour'. (*Bert Treep*)

Left: Andy Latimer in Groningen in 2013, the Lord of Understatement: 'I'm the sort of musician that can play anything – not necessarily well, but I can get a tune out of it!' (*Bert Treep*)

Right: Denis Clement, a picture of concentration, holding the beat in Amsterdam, 2013. (*Bert Treep*)

Left: *Night of the Prog 2015* and a contented Ton Scherpenzeel in one of his favourite spots: playing keys for Camel. (*Bert Treep*)

Right: At one with his instrument: Latimer at Night Of The Prog in 2015. (*Bert Treep*)

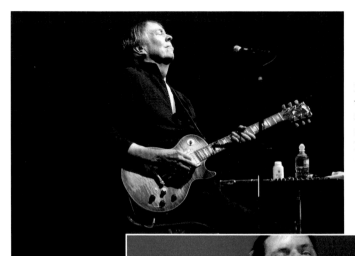

Left: Latimer with his treasured Sunburst Les Paul at Night Of The Prog in 2018. (*Bert Treep*)

Right: Peter Jones stunning the audience with his incredible sax solo during 'Rajaz' at Night Of The Prog in 2018. (*Bert Treep*)

Left: The band take their bows at Night Of The Prog, Loreley in 2018. 'Thank you, Loreley, and see you at the Royal Albert Hall in October'. (*Bert Treep*)

Right: 'Andy Latimer will be a guitar hero ranking with Clapton, Beck and Page', said the *NME* on the basis of his performance and this photo from the Royal Albert Hall in 2018, it looks like they were right after all. (*Geir Stavseng*)

Left: Bass, Clement and Latimer rocking out during 'Chord Change' at the Royal Albert Hall in 2018. (*Geir Stavseng*)

Right: A historic band in a historic setting: The Royal Albert Hall, 2018. (*Geir Stavseng*)

Left: *Rajaz*, the band's 1999 album, which included influences from North Africa. (*Camel Productions*)

Right: *A Nod And A Wink*, 2002. To date, this is Camel's last album of new material. (*Camel Productions*)

Left: *The Snow Goose*. The band re-recorded their classic album in 2013, with some tasteful embellishments. (*Camel Productions*)

Right: *A Live Record*. The band's superb live album was first released in 1978, and given the expanded treatment for a new CD release in 2002. (*Decca*)

Left: *Harbour Of Tears* tour ticket for the Astoria, London gig in 1997. The Astoria was infamous for the 'yellow river' that band members had to ford between the dressing room and stage. (*Private collection of Shane Carlson*)

Below: A ticket from the first of the 2003 Paradiso gigs in Amsterdam on the 'Farewell' tour in 2003. (*Private collection of Shane Carlson*)

FAN FARE presents

CAMEL

AT
LONDON ASTORIA
157 CHARING CROSS ROAD
LONDON WC2
SUNDAY 13th APRIL 1997
DOORS: 7pm · TICKETS £10.00 ADVANCE

01410

PARADISO
CAMEL

do 19 juni 2003   20.30 uur

ONGEPLACEERD   EUR 25,00
                        Toeslag EUR 3,00

LIDMAATSCHAP VERPLICHT   TSTA

97566   2
117894

Above: Latimer and Hoover's house overlooking the Pacific Ocean in Pescadero, CA, with Little Barn Studios, home of *Rajaz* and *A Nod And A Wink,* on the right. (*Photo courtesy of Dennis Mayer*)

NEVER LET GO
(Latimer) (From the LP "Camel" MUPS 473)

℗ 1973 MCA
Records Inc

mca

mca

CAMEL
Produced by Dave Williams
Engineer Roger Quested

Above: The single that started it all: the 1973 pressing of 'Never Let Go', with 'Curiosity' as the B-Side. (*Private collection of Shane Carlson*)

Three Wishes
Echoes
Another Night
Ice
Chord Change
Bobbins
The Hour Candle

Refugee
Fingertips
Slow Yourself Down
Rajaz
Sahara
Mother Road
Little Rivers
Hopeless Anger

Thanks from the sweets!

Left: Setlist from the 2 October 2000 gig at JB's in Dudley, England, on the *Rajaz* tour. Bass apparently enjoyed the confectionary provided by the fan in question. (*Private collection of Shane Carlson*)

'Elke' (Latimer)

Like *Moonmadness*, a lot of thought went into the track order for *Rain Dances*, evidenced here by the stark change of pace from the previous number to 'Elke'. Track ordering often goes un-noticed by listeners, because when it's 'right', it's to all intents invisible – think *Dark Side of the Moon, Sergeant Pepper* and *Moving Pictures;* however, when it's screwed up – boy, can it ruin an album as Genesis did by slicing and dicing the *Duke* suite – a mistake they subsequently corrected on tour. So, back to 'Elke', my point is that this song sits perfectly in the ordering of this LP. If you have a spare minute, create a playlist with 'Elke' anywhere else in the order: it just doesn't 'work'.

Production theory lesson over, back to the music. As with 'Tell Me' and 'Highway(s) of/to the Sun', again, we have a style previously unheard in the Camel canon. The ambient opening three minutes are, of course, all Brian Eno, here seen consciously loading his metaphorical palette for the classic *Ambient 1: Music for Airports* released the following year. Eno was introduced to Camel through *Rain Dances* producer Rhett Davies and was the ingredient that solidified Latimer's mental picture of the song, which would likely have been an incongruous solo spot in an otherwise group album.

Latimer's restrained flute is beautifully realised, and the layers of music – there's something like ten different instruments in the mix, including a harp – come together like a warm patchwork quilt of sound. In a radio interview with Shane Carlson in 2006 on ARfm, Andy Ward describes the song as 'haunting', which is a perfect descriptor.

'Elke' deserves repeated close and careful listens to work out what comes when – try it; it's a worthwhile experience. For such a keyboard-led piece, it's notable that Bardens was not credited as a co-writer: this is one of the first cracks starting to appear in the Latimer-Bardens partnership's hitherto incredible writing chemistry. In the same 2006 interview, Ward recounts that there were indeed some 'clandestine' goings-on, with Eno sneaked into the studio without Bardens' knowledge. When Bardens found out, he was understandably pissed off.

'Skylines' (Latimer, Bardens, Ward)

'Skylines' is the second of the *Rain Dances* tracks where Latimer played (fretless) bass as a consequence of his worrying that the now-departed Ferguson wouldn't be up to the job. Up to that point, Sinclair also was a purely fretted bass player, but as he would need to play fretless on the tour, he soon became proficient on the instrument, and it's been a feature of his playing ever since: thank you, Camel. Nevertheless, it's Latimer on fretless on the LP – and jolly good are his bass chops to boot.

Like 'One of These Days ...' earlier on the album, this is pure jazz-rock fusion, powered along by a selection of insistent bass riffs that don't miss a beat for the whole four and a half minutes: as the sleeve notes detail, 'sore fingers' indeed, for Mr Latimer. It's a showcase too for Bardens' synth work;

a couple of minutes in, he plays an extended Chick Corea-esque solo on two Minimoogs.

Ward is also clearly having a whale of a time on the drum stool, and as he had the previous year sat in on percussion with Brand X (for a single, rather memorable gig – see the Interlude in a moment), and as a co-writer on this number, it's not surprising that 'Skylines' is the most 'Brand X-y' of Camel's fusion-influenced output.

'Rain Dances' (Latimer, Bardens)

And so endeth the record, with the instrumental title track. The intro is certainly solemn – possibly even a little morbid and dirge-y, the gloomy atmosphere accentuated by Mel Collins on a melancholic-sounding soprano sax. Happily, the mood soon changes and *Rain Dances* picks up pace in the second two-thirds, which comprise arpeggiated 'pizzicato' guitar overlaying string and other synths, unsupported by either bass or drums (Ward and Sinclair contributing nothing, apparently, but umbrellas), using a variation to reprise the 'First Light' theme. The overall effect recalls side one of *Tubular Bells*, especially the pizzicato guitar and although it's a pleasant enough way to sign off the record, it's hardly vintage stuff. The sleeve notes refer to Latimer using a 'treated piano', but despite listening to this track over and over, I just can't fathom out what part that instrument plays. Unlike some other Camel LPs, this time the best wasn't left until last.

Interlude: Andy Ward Adds A Special Ingredient Of His Own to Brand X

Interviewed by Mick Dillingham of the *Art Into Dust* blog in 2002, Ward tells the story of the genesis of Phil Collins' collaboration on *I Can See Your House From Here*, as well as recounting his calamitous one-off collaboration with Brand X one night in 1976.

I first met Phil Collins while we were recording Mirage, at Basing Street studios. Genesis were downstairs in the larger studio putting the finishing touches to Lamb Lies Down [this was recording Gabriel's vocals and post-production as the instrumental recording sessions took place in Wales] and I needed to borrow a drum key. So we got chatting and Phil was a very friendly guy; we met a couple more times after that, exchanged phone numbers and that sort of thing.

Then Gabriel did his famous split from Genesis, and I did a major interview with Chris Welch in Melody Maker, and the subject of Genesis came up, and he ended up using that as the headline 'Andy Ward says Genesis will survive without Gabriel', which was kind of odd, you know, as if I knew! It turned out that Phil really was a strong singer, and the rest is history, as they say. But at the time it really pleased him, so the next time I saw him he was really chuffed, 'Hey, thanks for the name check', because it was really positive publicity at a time when they needed it.

Anyway, soon after, he phoned me and asked me would I like to play percussion with his jazz rock band, Brand X, at a gig in London? I said 'I'd love to', I was very excited by this, so I went along and rehearsed with them. I found them quite something to follow, not knowing the tunes, and there were a lot of time changes, very demanding. I picked up on a few things, good enough to do the gig, but I was quite nervous about it. Anyway, the next day came, and it was the gig, at a place called The Nashville in London. It had a tiny little stage, with the five of us crammed on; I was set up directly behind Phil Collins on another little platform.

We started playing and everything was going swimmingly well for twenty minutes or so, but during the fourth number, I was playing tambourine with my right hand, and occasionally hitting cymbals with it, and catching them with my left hand to choke the sound. I did a particularly spirited one of these and failed to catch the cymbal with my left hand; the result was the cymbal crashed directly onto Phil's left shoulder. Which I'd imagine was quite painful, it was just the most awful moment, and he gave me a very cold look that froze me to the floor.

We carried on playing, but I felt pretty shaken and was being very careful, but lo and behold, it happened again! This time I missed Phil but demolished half his drumkit and this time, the band had to stop playing altogether while things were put right. The rest of the band thought it very funny and made a thing of it during the announcements. I was never asked to play with them again. But they were a great band, and it was a fun evening except for those two incidents.

Tony Brainsby Publicity
105 Winchester Street London SW1
01-834 8341/4   Home: 589 3961

NEW MEMBERS FOR CAMEL

Owing to increasing musical differences, Peter Bardens has left Camel. The split is amicable.

The group has just completed recording a new album with Peter called "Breathless", for release to coincide with the first leg of a major seven month world tour that takes Camel from the UK to Europe, the States, and Japan.

For this tour, Camel - Andrew Latimer (guitar); Andy Ward (drums); Richard Sinclair (bass) - will be joined by Mel Collins on saxophone, Dave Sinclair on keyboards, and Jan Schelhass also on keyboards. Mel Collins has previously worked with Camel, on their last two albums and tours. The band are currently in intensive rehearsals.

Peter Bardens has already recorded an album with Van Morrison for release later this year, and will be working on various new musical projects.

Andrew Latimer says: "Obviously the parting has a certain sadness about it but we now have a new energy to move the band a stage further. We're really looking forward to touring again after ten months off the road."

Camel were formed six years ago and have sold over two million albums, the last three studio LPs having been Top Twenty hits.

July 1978.

TONY BRAINSBY PUBLICITY LTD. DIRECTORS: TONY BRAINSBY JANE BRAINSBY
REGISTERED OFFICE: 40 WELBECK STREET W1   COMPANY NO.: 060735 VAT NO. 239 0519 22

Above: And then there were three - no, six: the old 'musical differences' chestnut is cited on Bardens' departure press release from 1978, also announcing the arrival of Dave Sinclair and Jan Schelhaas. (*Private collection of Shane Carlson*)

Breathless (1978)

Personnel:
Andrew Latimer: guitar, vocals
Peter Bardens: keyboards, vocals
Richard Sinclair: bass, vocals
Andy Ward: drums, percussion
Mel Collins: Saxes, flute, oboe
Additional musicians
Dave Sinclair: synthesizer on 'You Make Me Smile', piano on 'Rainbow's End'
Jan Schelhaas: clavinet on 'You Make Me Smile'
Produced by Mick Glossop and Camel at The Manor, Chipping Norton, England
Engineered by Mick Glossop
Release date: 22 September 1978
Running time: 44:56
Current edition: Esoteric Recordings CD ECLEC 2155
Highest chart places: UK: 26, USA: 134

Breathless came together when the band returned from touring *Rain Dances* in the USA and although there had been tensions between Bardens and Latimer, they decided to give their writing partnership a reboot, so again headed to the countryside, this time to Cornwall in the far southwest of England.

Latimer says the time spent there was quite enjoyable as both rediscovered that they got on really well while collaborating on new music. However, when the rubber hit the road and it was time to go into the studio, the songs they had written weren't working when the rest of the band came into the picture. The rift between Latimer and Bardens resurfaced, becoming clearly apparent to the others. Latimer recalled in a 1981 interview with American broadcaster Mal Reding:

> Peter and I were just stifling each other. I wouldn't let him get any of his ideas out, and he wouldn't let me get any of mine out, so the feeling in the studio was pretty heavy weather. We were always arguing – about what instrument should take a solo and what sort of sound should go into the mix. And in those sorts of situations, nobody's right or wrong; it's just a different point of view.

Apparently, there was also tension brewing between Bardens and Sinclair, who, along with Ward, was pushing for a jazzier direction in the band. Add to this that even though officially the bass player was a full-time member, his real ambition was to go solo and as such, he never fully bought into the Camel family. 'Richard had his own agenda', says Latimer on *CV*.

Ultimately Bardens and the band decided to part company. Reassuringly, though, the split with Latimer was on a professional level only. Their friendship was lifelong, maintaining regular social contact particularly when both found themselves living in California.

So, not for the last time in the band's history, the search was on to find a keyboard player – this time to both help finish the record and go on the road. By coincidence, Caravan had just gone on hiatus after releasing an album that was rockier than was usual for the band in *Better By Far*, produced by star knob-twiddler Tony Visconti who had only months before worked on *Low* with David Bowie: the proverbial lightbulb started to flicker above Sinclair's head.

At that point in time, Caravan had two keyboard players in tow, and these ivory tinklers were likely staring into the gainful employment abyss. Phone calls were made, chins were scratched, and duly Richard's cousin David and Jan Schelhaas joined the fray.

David was the writer of Caravan's unquestionable masterpiece, 'Nine Feet Underground', and previously had played in the ground-breaking Wilde Flowers with Kevin Ayers and Robert Wyatt, so his credentials were plain for all to see. Likewise, Schelhaas had a pedigree going back to the late 60s, including collaborations with Gary Moore of Thin Lizzy fame and future Uriah Heep drum man Lee Kerslake. Due to Bardens' sudden departure, both players ended up contributing to the album as well as touring.

After the run of recordings at Basing Street – from *Mirage* to *Rain Dances* – the band headed out of London (and away from direct Decca interference) to the picturesque Cotswolds and Richard Branson's The Manor Studio. With the change of studio, there also came a change of producer, with Mick Glossop now in charge of the tape, buttons and sliders. Glossop was a fixture at The Manor and had engineered Tangerine Dream's *Rubycon* (1975) and *Ricochet* (also 1975) for Virgin, so had form in the progressive sphere. Although this would be the only time he worked with Camel, from a prog fan's perspective, it's good to know that he was also the engineer behind Frank Zappa's astonishing triple album *Shut Up 'n' Play Yer Guitar* from 1981.

Although he had the aforementioned itchy feet, Richard Sinclair was nonetheless embedded in the line-up and takes the microphone on three of the seven vocal tracks, Latimer singing on the other four, percentage-wise making this the most vocal-led and radio-friendly Camel album so far, no doubt bringing smiles to the faces of the record company and A&R people.

With the album came Camel's most extensive ever tour, spanning September 1978 to February 1979 and taking in the UK and continental Europe, Japan and the USA, ending with a historic four-day residency at LA's legendary Roxy Theatre on Sunset Strip.

Previous album *Rain Dances* did relatively well in the album charts, peaking at 20, and *Breathless* performed almost to that level with the buying public, reaching 26 in the UK album charts. Like the previous LP, it's an eclectic mix of styles, and to my mind, contains only one vintage Camel classic, 'Echoes', and one fusion tour-de-force in 'The Sleeper'. *Breathless*, therefore, remains the proverbial Curate's Egg: good, in parts.

'Breathless' (Latimer, Bardens, Ward)

Rain Dances ended with the title track, which might have confused some people, so *Breathless* starts in a more conventional manner. The first of the Sinclair vocal tracks, his voice is certainly the purest so far in the Camel catalogue – no running of the mic through a phaser or fuzzbox here. The singing is backed by some restrained acoustic guitar and flowing bass lines, with the drums sitting far back in the mix. The highlight of 'Breathless' is the lovely use of an oboe as a counterpoint to the main melody. Lyrically, 'Breathless' is a proper love song, but the music doesn't stray into ballad territory, which is a refreshing approach. The title track ends with a beautiful coda where Latimer's flute joins in with the oboe; so far, so good.

'Echoes' (Latimer, Bardens, Ward)

It wasn't in character for Camel to get political, but on 'Echoes', they do by telling the story of the Navajo 'Long March' that took place in the spring of 1864. The US Army forced around 9,000 Navajo men, women and children, to walk over 300 miles through the desert to Fort Sumner, New Mexico, to be interned at the infamous Bosque Redondo. The internment was disastrous for the Navajo, as the government failed to provide an adequate supply of water, firewood, provisions and livestock; today the Navajo refer to this period as 'The Fearing Time'.

For such a harrowing tale, the music is surprisingly upbeat: the overture gallops along at a fair pace before slowing down into an airy synth-led section, coupled with some neat guitar work, then bass and drums gradually fading in before the main 'Echoes' theme comes magnificently to the fore, Sinclair's complex bass lines adding great depth to the sound.

With another change of pace and theme, the first and second verses, sung by Latimer, tell the story detailed above from the perspective of the ghosts of those who died on the trek and subsequent internment. Now comes the guitar-led instrumental bridge, featuring an uplifting extended solo that segues into the final verse, closing with a full band jam. Once more, we see the band's talent for coherent, multi-section writing that, although far removed from the template of 'verse, chorus, verse, chorus, bridge' and so on, still hangs together without overwhelming the listener with complexity. 'Echoes' sits firmly in my Camel top ten.

'Wing And A Prayer' (Latimer, Bardens)

Quirky and tongue-in-cheek in style, Bardens takes on lead vocal duties for the only time on *Breathless*. 'Wing and a Prayer' is a bit of a let-down after the immensity of 'Echoes', but so be it. Lightweight as the song may be, 'Wing and a Prayer' is a great example of ensemble playing and the layered lyrics are great fun to listen to, making this a tasty slice of pop-prog to bop along to on a sunny Sunday morning. On the subject of Sunday mornings …

'Down On The Farm' (Sinclair)

It's no surprise that this slice of English Canterbury-infused progressive rock whimsy was penned by Richard Sinclair. As the sole Sinclair-only written track on the album, heaven knows what cajoling went on with the rest of the band to get it committed to vinyl, but thank goodness it was, as it's a cracker – even though I'm sure I'm not alone in thinking that this one was leftover in his notebook from the Caravan days. Without mincing words, it's 'Golf Girl' with cows, chicken, sheep … and lingerie.

Nevertheless, there are few tracks in the canon of English rock music that capture the comic air of the countryside quite like this. 'Sneak out the back way with Nellie the barmaid' and farmer's daughters hanging up their undies, indeed. But at the same time, especially in the opening chords, it really rocks, with Latimer strumming out power chords and screeching up and down the fretboard like some amped-up shredder.

By dint of its catchiness and straight-up slapstick, this is the one I'd have chosen to be a single. Sure, it's about as far away from the real Camel as you can get, but as an entry point for new buyers, it almost certainly would have done the trick. However, I suspect that as earnest band members, it was probably this novelty element that scotched that possibility, although Father Abraham & The Smurfs, 10cc's 'Dreadlock Holiday' and the dirge of 'Matchstalk Men & Matchstalk Cats & Dogs' all hit the Top Ten in the UK in 1978, so what do I know?

All in all, a fun and light-hearted charabanc excursion out of town, but maybe a day trip too far as Camel didn't return to those Elysian fields, hedgerows and trout-filled streams until *A Nod and a Wink* 24 years later.

'Starlight Ride' (Latimer, Bardens)

If we can agree on the simile that 'Wing and a Prayer' is lightweight, then 'Starlight Ride' is the lower end of flyweight. Sadly, the best I can say about this ditty is that it's clearly well arranged and very Bach-y when the woodwind comes forward in the mix, but apart from that, it's quite forgettable. The personal tension building between Latimer and Bardens was clearly having an effect on their writing as there is simply no equivalence between this and, say, 'Song Within A Song' or even 'Echoes' earlier on the LP. It's always traumatic to watch a break-up, but this is exactly what we're witnessing right now. Camel had triumphed over the 'difficult second album syndrome', but fate finally caught up with them on LP number six.

'Summer Lightning' (Latimer, Sinclair)

Camel go disco? I'm afraid so, people, and this is the point at which *Breathless* really looks in danger of coming off the rails, the sole saving grace being Latimer's wonderful and stylistically bang on Nile Rodgers-esque closing solo. Words fail me when trying to describe how incongruous and at odds this track is compared with the best of Camel's output. But I'll try: apart from that solo and some great keys work, it's disposable, embarrassing, dad dancing fodder. Shame. Bardens had nothing to do with the writing of this one, which I'm sure, given the circumstances, brought a *schadenfreude* grin to his face once the reviews started coming in.

'You Make Me Smile' (Latimer, Bardens)

After being subjected to the previous number, the squelchy bass intro to 'You Make Me Smile', recalling as it does countless sausage machine dance numbers of the 70s, strikes fear into one's heart that we're in for more of the same cod-disco drivel. Thankfully the band just about steal victory out of defeat by a combination of good humour and a really catchy melody.

With Bardens now MIA, both Schelhaas and Dave Sinclair contributed to 'You Make Me Smile' in the studio with some overdubs, the former on clavinet and the latter on synths, but you would hard-pressed to notice.

For sure, this is in no way 24-carat Camel, but the bounciness and lyrical content save the day – who doesn't love someone that can make them smile? Bardens' Moog solo in the bridge, laid down before his departure, is a gem too. A Pyrrhic Victory, maybe, but a win all the same.

'The Sleeper' (Latimer, Bardens, Ward, Mel Collins)

At last! Thank the Flying Spaghetti Monster (or insert your deity of choice)! Hidden away as the penultimate track, Camel's fusion talents are laid out in tremendous fashion. 'The Sleeper' is another Brand X-influenced, fantastically funky and accomplished jazz-rock composition. It just loses out to 'Echoes' as the longest track on *Breathless*, but so joyous is it that I'd happily lap up a double portion of this.

All the required genre elements are present and correct in this sophisticated take on fusion: Fender Rhodes piano, vibrato Moog work, athletic bass lines, chorused sax, tricky time signatures – and even a polyrhythm can be heard throughout with Ward's precision muted cymbal playing. Latimer's solo is on a par with anything Al de Meola and his contemporaries were churning out at the time, so again I find it a tragically missed opportunity that fusion fans overlooked this material.

'Rainbow's End' (Latimer, Bardens)

Chosen as the sole 45rpm release from the album, but not until it was combined with 'Remote Romance' and 'Tell Me' as the 'maxi' single supporting the release of *I Can See Your House From Here*, 'Rainbow's End' marks not only the end of the album but also the end of another era. Apart from a cameo role on *The Single Factor*, and his surprise three-number appearance in Hammersmith on the *Stationary Traveller* tour, this is the last time we'd hear Bardens with Camel, and he hardly goes out with a bang which, considering the circumstances, was probably for the best.

I Can See Your House From Here (1979)

Personnel:
Andrew Latimer: guitar, vocals
Kit Watkins: keyboards, flute
Jan Schelhaas: keyboards
Colin Bass: bass, vocals
Andy Ward: drums, percussion
Additional musicians
Mel Collins: alto sax
Phil Collins: percussion
Rupert Hine: backing vocals
Simon Jeffes: orchestral arrangements
Produced by Camel and Rupert Hine at Farmyard Studios, Little Chalfont, England,
Summer 1979
Engineer: Peter Kelsey and Richard Austen
Release date: 29 October 1979
Running time: 46:04
Current edition: Esoteric Records ECLEC 2158
Highest chart places: UK: 45, USA: did not chart

And then there were two.

Originally entitled *Endangered Species*, a relatively harmless slice of self-parody, it's hard to fathom why the band changed its mind and chose to use the punchline of a rather tasteless joke as the title of the new album, let alone why they then doubled down and signed-off on a cover that was inevitably going to get all of Christendom steamed up – especially in the potential sales goldmine of the USA. Oh, that cover. As if the band hadn't learned their lessons from the early days regarding courting controversy and as if they weren't acutely familiar with the peculiarities of the US record-buying public. Nevertheless, they decided to go with a record sleeve, based on a rather tasteless joke that was doing the rounds in England's pubs and clubs around that time, showing a crucified astronaut orbiting the Earth. Ooh, boy.

Amazingly there was no second cover for the US release, where, incidentally, the album didn't chart. I know that correlation does not imply causation, but you have to wonder. However, the South African distributor opted to play it safe with the God-fearing record-buying public, and so that pressing has its own, frankly messy but much sought-after by collectors, sleeve.

I Can See Your House from Here is a transitional record in many ways. For starters, it's the first without Bardens, and many at the time – fans and pundits alike – would posit that this spelt the beginning of the end for the band. 'Irreplaceable', 'he was the soul of Camel', 'he wrote half the songs' and similar comments echoed around the business. To fill the Bardens-shaped hole in the band, as we know from the *Breathless* story, Latimer had recruited not one, but two new keys players, Schelhaas and Sinclair, bringing a new and exciting dynamic, especially on stage. However, Dave Sinclair, as well as cousin Richard, had headed for pastures new, so another, second, keyboardist was recruited in the form of Happy the Man's Kit Watkins.

Secondly, the pressure from Decca for a hit single – or even a number that could be touted to the radio stations – was continuing to be a thorn in the side of Camel's creative process. With a couple of tracks, Latimer seemed to have taken this on board, and then with 'Remote Romance', overboard.

In spite of such stylistic aberrations, however, Camel returned to their foundational prog and fusion roots on many of the cuts. *I Can See Your House From Here* also benefits from lush and expansive orchestral arrangements, led by Simon Jeffes of avant-pop vanguards Penguin Café Orchestra. A particular highlight of this was on 'Who We Are', although sometimes maybe going a little too far as, for example, with 'Survival'. All of the orchestral overdubs on 'Who We Are' and 'Survival' were laid down at A.I.R. Studios in London.

Main recording took place in yet another studio new to Camel, this time at Rupert Hine's Farmyard Studios in leafy Buckinghamshire. At the end of the 1970s, Hine was a respected producer, with credits including Kevin Ayers, Dave Greenslade and Ant Phillips, but to the average man in the street he is probably best remembered as keyboard player in the band Quantum Jump. Around the time of recording, *I Can See Your House From Here* Hine's band had experienced unexpected one-hit-wonder chart success in the UK with the novelty song, 'Lone Ranger' ('Taumatawhakatangihangakoauauotamateapokaiwhenuakitanatahu', and all that).

Hine's star was to rise high in the production firmament in the 80s and 90s, with artists including Rush (*Presto* and *Roll the Bones*), Saga (*Worlds Apart* and *Heads or Tales*), Tina Turner (*Break Every Rule* and *Foreign Affair*), Chris de Burgh (*Man On The Line*), The Thompson Twins (*Close To The Bone*) and Stevie Nicks (*The Other Side of the Mirror*) all beating a path to his door. Latimer clearly enjoyed the collaboration, stating on *CV*:

> Rupert was great fun to work with; he was really up and zappy. I enjoyed making that record. We did it rather quickly and it wasn't a lengthy production.

With the departure of Richard Sinclair, it was time for bass player number three. Laurie Small, tour manager for Steve Hillage, was friends with the band and introduced them to Colin Bass, who had recently been part of Hillage's live set up on the tour for *L*. The guys met up at rehearsal studio Wood Farm in Suffolk, and immediately Bass wanted in. From *CV*:

> It sounded fantastic, as I sat down and played with them I thought 'this is great – I'd like to be part of that'. Luckily, I got the job.

Mel Collins also joined in for one song, playing an alto sax solo on 'Your Love Is Stranger Than Mine', but did not tour the album due to a multitude of commitments with artists such as Sally Oldfield, Joan Armatrading and Gerry Rafferty.

However, it's 'the other Collins' who was a major contributor, although you wouldn't know from the original sleeve notes that state simply: '… for his demon percussion and aural concussion', with no individual track credits. Yes: that Collins – Phil, to be exact, who as we already know from earlier on, was chums with Andy Ward. Maybe he joined on percussion to get revenge for that fateful Brand X gig!

Anyway, we have direct and unambiguous first-hand evidence of the extent of Collins, P's contribution on good authority, as Jan Schelhaas recalled in conversation with Esoteric Records' Mark Powell in 2008:

Although Phil Collins claims to not remember doing the session, he did – I was there! He came along with a massive van full of his percussion stuff and I think he literally played on every track – he seemed to be enjoying it at the time.

Rounding off the collaborators, two musicians provided lyrics but no playing. John McBurnie ('Wait') was an English guitarist and vocalist who had collaborated on LPs with Michael Chapman. Chapman supported Camel on the *Breathless* tour and through him, McBurnie remained in touch. Vivienne 'Viv' McAuliffe ('Neon Magic') is best known as the lead singer of English jazz-rock fusion band Affinity, who were active for a few years on either side of 1970. From a progressive rock standpoint, though, the pair were integral to Patrick Moraz's 1976 classic, *The Story Of i*, *Keyboard* magazine's Best Keyboard Album of the Year, with McBurnie as lead vocalist and lyricist and McAuliffe supplying backing vocals. Further cementing the interconnections with Camel, McAuliffe also sang on Ant Phillips' *Geese And The Ghost*, and as we shall see later on, Ant has a large part to play in this story.

Ultimately, the album is a great listen and is undoubtedly 'proper' Camel, with or without Bardens' guiding light. It's also, of course, the first LP with Colin Bass on bass, the start of his (at time of writing) wonderful 42-year association with the band.

Camel toured the album in Europe in November and December of 1979, and then in January the following year, headed again to the Land Of The Rising Sun, Japan, playing a total of five gigs in Tokyo and Nagoya. On said tour, for my first and only time at a Camel gig, a schoolfriend and I sat front and centre at the Birmingham Odeon – holding the mythical white tickets marked 'A12' and 'A13'. How I ended up with those tickets is a long and heart-warming story, but this isn't the place to recount it. Instead, send my publisher a mail which I'm sure he'll pass on and then I'll give you chapter and verse.

Although reckoned by many fans and critics to be one of the weakest of all Camel albums, I confess to having a rather large soft spot for *I Can See Your*

House, 'Wait', 'Who We Are', 'Hymn to Her' and of course the triumphant 'Ice' more than make up for the somewhat below par quality of the other tracks. As an EP, it would be regarded as a masterpiece.

'Wait' (Latimer, McBurnie)

Co-written by Latimer (music) and John McBurnie (lyrics), 'Wait' is a tremendous opener, full of energy, joie-de-vivre and chops galore – typical Rupert Hine, in fact. I'm a sucker for side one, track one in a major key – 'Going for the One' and 'Tom Sawyer' in particular spring to mind – and 'Wait' is a corker in this respect. It's always better to start off upbeat, I think, like smiling when you enter a room full of people. There's no build-up here – we're straight into it, no messing about – and wallop, off we go at 170bpm!

Opening with the guitarist soloing over that frantic beat, Latimer's vocals quickly enter the equation to tell the story of a presumably unlucky card player in a casino. It's unknown if this was autobiographical on the lyricist's part.

After a couple more minutes of versing, chorusing and generally rocking out, including a couple of heroic pick slides/scratches from Latimer thrown in for good measure, we get to the highlight of 'Wait': the 'duelling Moogs' of Schelhaas and Watkins. What a blast this section is, top-drawer soloing on the storied gizmos. The keyboardists really wanted us to know who was doing what too, as the sleeve notes quite explicitly state that Watkins is responsible for solos one and three, and Schelhaas the evens: so now you know.

Live, this pairing was even better, walking a tightrope where one bum note, mistiming, or accidental heavy-handedness on the pitch-bend wheel would have had the whole thing tumbling ungracefully into a safety net.

Once the pyrotechnics on the 'black 'n' whites' has ended, it's back to a reprise of the main theme and an intricate Latimer extended solo that gently fades away, leaving us wanting more.

'Your Love Is Stranger Than Mine' (Latimer, Ward, Schelhaas, Bass)

There was a Canterbury-influenced undercurrent in the previous two records and even though the Sinclair cousins were gone, this gets another airing with 'Your Love Is Stranger Than Mine' – a poppy, light-hearted, singalong and riff-laden number spiced up by some fun instrumental bon-mots and an infectious beat.

Very much keyboard-led, the spacey riff that recurs throughout the number is Watkins on the recently introduced and legendary Sequential Circuits Prophet 5 synth, an early model of which was literally sitting on a pedestal in Hine's studio: he only got to use it on this track, such was its eminence.

Vocal duty is taken up for the first time by Colin Bass, and he sounds great, hitting the high notes without effort. For once, Latimer takes a background role both vocally and on the six-string and the outro is overlaid by a quality jazzy sax solo from Mel C.

'Your Love Is Stranger Than Mine' was released as a single in the UK in February 1980 with 'Neon Magic' as the B-Side, but – surprise, surprise – although it got some valuable radio play, it didn't chart.

'Eye Of The Storm' (Watkins)
A bit of an oddity, this, as it's a leftover from Watkins' Happy the Man days. It certainly has the Camel feel, but somehow it seems out of place on its own. I get the impression that this was an early experiment that would inform the more symphonic vein of *Nude.* It seems that Watkins pressed it to be included as it was a solo work and he wanted to underline his credentials as a composer. Certainly, if you intercut it into *Nude* – between 'Drafted' and 'Docks', for example – it sits there innocuously enough and fits the mood perfectly.

Musically, 'Eye of the Storm' is a pastoral interlude combining gentle acoustic guitar and Watkins' restrained flute and keyboards, underpinned by some quality fretless bass in the hands of Bass. In fact, this period at the Farmyard was a pivotal moment in the bass player's evolution, as Colin recalled in conversation with me early in 2021:

Rupert Hine introduced me to Wal basses, so I bought a couple and that really upped my game as a bass player.

Continuing much in the same orchestral vein, the song fades out accompanied by Ward's 'massed marching military snares' and Watkins' multi-tracked martial flute – both of which clearly presage 'The Homecoming' on *Nude.*

'Who We Are' (Latimer)
'Who We Are' is a ballad with a difference, and as cinematic as Camel get – a Technicolor, Panavision extravaganza, given extra dimensions thanks to the lavish orchestrations courtesy of Simon Jeffes. Billy Connolly's favourite instrument, the autoharp, gets an airing right from the get-go, with Latimer also playing a snappy chorused lead over the top and Schelhaas tinkling the ivories at the grand piano. It's a delightful and uplifting opening section that, after two minutes, changes mood as the vocals enter with a tale of a lonely musician on the road and missing his partner, slipping in a sly reference to maybe straying a little groupie-wise in the process.

Then there's a short bridge with an acoustic guitar sounding exquisite, then another verse and chorus interspersed with some of the aforementioned orchestrations leading to a false ending. Luckily for us, there's more to come as the orchestra increases pace and dynamics, the band seamlessly joining in for a final couple of choruses and some cute keyboard runs from Watkins.

'Who We Are' is the only bona fide multi-section work on the album, and every piece fits together beautifully. Its almost eight minutes are over all too soon.

'Survival' (Latimer)

As a standalone, purely orchestral track, 'Survival' seems to me to be little more than unnecessary packing, polystyrene peanuts, if you will, filling in the crevices of the deeper cuts. As an overture to 'Hymn to Her', it works a little better, although this being the case, why wasn't it incorporated into that? We'll probably never know, but if you do – send me a postcard.

'Hymn To Her' (Latimer, Schelhaas)

As the title suggests, 'Hymn to Her' is undoubtedly choral in style. OK, its not exactly Handel's *Messiah*, but it does have that expansive atmosphere of a cathedral setting, with a foundation of multi-layered string synths amplifying the effect: shame there wasn't a Mellotron available as well. Conceived by Schelhaas, speaking to Mark Powell in 2008, he said he approached Latimer with the idea:

> Writing with Andy was a very natural thing; we were on the same wavelength at that particular time. For no apparent reason, it just seemed to gel. When I played 'Hymn to Her', he latched onto it straight away.

Starting in epic fashion with Latimer soloing over the aforementioned strings and a grand piano, when the lyrics come in, it's clear we have another love song, but this time without the groupies. Latimer is at the limit of his register but acquits himself well.

Then, almost exactly halfway through what has so far been a lovely but pretty standard ballad, 'Hymn to Her' really takes off in a totally unexpected direction, again showcasing Camel's ability to surprise. Wow. Latimer brilliantly channels Fotheringay, Fairports and Gerry Rafferty man Jerry Donahue's trademark string bending in the middle section and Ward's Rototom drum fills are a joy, keyboards and bass perfectly filling in the gaps.

With a return to the main theme, we're done. This is a real live favourite, for good reason, and it's worth pondering whether an edited single version of 'Hymn to Her' could well have been the hit Camel never had.

Wrapping up on 'Hymn to Her', please permit me a small nerdy diversion, as I think the musos amongst us will be interested and have an opinion. The pizzicato strings we hear at the two-minute mark are not orchestral overdubs but, it seems to me, Watkins' and Hine's clever use of a modulated ARP Solina overdubbed with Hammond – an innovative solution.

'Neon Magic' (Latimer, McAuliffe, Schelhaas)

Latimer snarling in a faux-angry voice and McAuliffe's faux-angry lyrics – more suited to Sham 69 or The Damned than Camel – make this one a real puzzle. Is it meant to be ironic? Is it caustic social commentary? Is the mishmash of styles meant to be an allegory of a mixed-up world? And what are those fairground organ noises at the end all about? Presumably a reference to 'neon', 'carousels', and bumper cars hitting and running, not a premonition of *Grand Theft Auto*. Why, Camel, why?

'Remote Romance' (Latimer, Watkins)
As if the preceding number wasn't worrying enough, 'Remote Romance' is quite possibly the most disposable of all Camel songs, period. Forty years later, I'm still bamboozled as to how this piece of seriously sub-standard Human League-pastiche electro-twaddle actually made it through the microphones, along the cables and into the mixing desk, let alone onto the finished LP. It's a makeweight so insignificant and pointless that it should best be forgotten, but it sits there on the LP like an angry red boil on the end of your nose, desperately needing to be lanced but stubbornly staying put. The only possible defence open to the band is that maybe all the new tech *Chez Hine* – sequencers, Vocoders and the like – just had to be tinkered with, and resistance was therefore futile. It was released as one of the songs on the maxi-single; it didn't trouble the chart compilers. Enough said.

'Ice' (Latimer)
After the execrably awful pseudo-new-wave-synthpop of 'Remote Romance', and the pointlessness of the song before that, listeners might be forgiven for thinking that *I Can See Your House From Here* was going to fizzle out with a whimper, leaving listeners in despair of what on earth had happened to their heroes' sense of musical direction. But instead, we got 'Ice'. Wonderful, amazing, incredible 'Ice'.

We begin our ten-minute musical journey with a grand piano (Watkins this time) and Les Paul duet of astounding beauty and breathtaking compositional accomplishment, and so all can breathe a deep sigh of relief. The previous two tracks were an aberration, normal service is resumed.

When the band come in, the scale of what we're about to hear is immediately apparent. The main theme, played by solo lead guitar in unison with the string synth, is a joy. There's a subtle Fender Rhodes tinkling in the background, and then that stunning, perfectly judged Minimoog solo from Watkins – showcasing just how foundational to prog the sounds from that piece of equipment were.

And now we attain Nirvana: is this Latimer's greatest solo of all time? I think more would say 'yes' than 'no'. The emotion, the precision, the technique – it's transcendental in all of its three-and-a-half-minute magnificence; a cadenza worthy of Paganini.

The closing two minutes, with lead guitar, floating over an acoustic backdrop that was added later – the only overdub on 'Ice' – is a fitting close to this unquestionable epic. Sometimes magic happens, and in the case of 'Ice' the pixie dust poured down on the studio in torrents – I still pinch myself when remembering that this was recorded live in one take.

Underlining the critical place the song holds in Camel's repertoire, this was the first song that Pete Jones – more of whom later – was asked to play for his audition, and it remains a cornerstone of the live set to this day. Magnificent.

Above: Ad from *Sounds* in September 1979 for the new album and UK tour, which duly sold out. (*Private collection of Shane Carlson*)

Nude (1981)

Personnel:
Andrew Latimer: guitars, vocals, flute, koto, keyboards
Colin Bass: bass, vocals
Andy Ward: drums, percussion
Additional musicians
Mel Collins: flute, piccolo, saxophones
Duncan Mackay: keyboards
Jan Schelhaas: piano on 'The Last Farewell'
Chris Green: cello on 'Drafted'
Gasper Lawal: percussion on 'Changing Places'
Herbie Flowers: tuba on 'The Homecoming'
Produced at: Abbey Road Studios by Camel, Tony Clarke and Haydn Bendall
Engineer: Tony Clarke
Release date: 31 January 1981
Running time: 44:45
Current edition: Esoteric Recordings ECLEC 2159
Highest chart places: UK: 34

Nude is a full-on return to form, always ranked highly in the fans' Camel hall of fame. Unlike *Breathless* and *I Can See Your House From Here*, the album is all of a piece stylistically and sees Camel replanting their melodic roots.

Nude is, of course, Camel's first concept album since *The Snow Goose*. Properly, I understand from a Japanese acquaintance, pronounced 'Noo-duh', on first listening, buyers might have been a little befuddled by the lack of content relating to bare skin, but Noo-duh it is. Musically, *Nude* points the way to the direction Latimer would head once he and Susan Hoover struck out on their own. It's an extended composition based on historical fact and not, as with *The Snow Goose*, on fictional characters. It was Hoover who pitched the story to Latimer, and he bought in immediately, saying on *CV*:

> Like Snow Goose, it was easy again for me to do as it has a story, characters, different things that happen in the plot. I find that very easy to do writing-wise; you get a very clear picture if the story or the emotion or whatever you're trying to do is strong.

To recap on that story, Nude – or Hiroo Onoda, to use his given name – was a Japanese army intelligence officer who, through missed communications, was unaware that WWII had ended, and believing that the war was ongoing continued, along with three compatriots, guerrilla operations on the Philippines island of Lubang. Although in October 1945, he and the others read a dropped leaflet stating that Japan had surrendered, they ignored the content believing this to be propaganda. By 1972, the last of his cohort was dead after a shoot-out with local police, and Nude was alone.

Eventually, after nearly 30 years in hiding and subsisting on the land, with occasional forays into villages to steal food, he met another Japanese, Norio Suzuki, who had made it his mission to find Nude. Australian public broadcaster, ABC, interviewed Onoda in 2010, where he said:

> This hippie boy Suzuki came to the island to listen to the feelings of a Japanese soldier. Suzuki asked me why I would not come out.

After a month of to-ing and fro-ing, with Nude refusing to surrender without official orders from a superior officer, the Japanese government eventually located his commanding officer from WWII, who flew to Lubang and presented him with the necessary orders.

I'll cover what happened after Nude's return to Japan in the track-by-track breakdown. Importantly, bear in mind that Hoover used quite a bit of artistic licence story-wise, as her narrative has Nude alone on the island from the word go. This shouldn't detract from the music, though.

Moving onto the recording, after a run of Top 40 albums, even without that coveted hit single, Decca decided to throw the dice and put significant money behind the effort. So, it was that for their eighth album Camel finally made it the Shangri La of studios – Abbey Road, home of The Beatles, *Dark Side Of The Moon* and Al Stewart's *Year Of The Cat*. On *CV* Andy Ward said of the facility:

> Recording at Abbey Road was a dream come true ... the engineers were superb.

And, also on *CV*, Latimer also remembers the time fondly:

> We were in the canteen and then Paul McCartney came and sat at our table and started drinking tea with us – so you try to be normal, but it's difficult.

A change of studio also brought yet another change of producer, this time Haydn Bendall who was the incumbent Chief Engineer at Abbey Road, working alongside Tony Clarke, who was best known for producing The Moody Blues from 1966 to 1979.

In case you were wondering, yes, you read the personnel listing above correctly: Latimer plays keyboards on Nude; who knew he had it in him? Duncan Mackay takes lead keyboard duty covering for Watkins and Schelhaas, who were unavailable for the sessions due to other commitments. Schelhaas however, did manage to contribute to one track, playing piano on 'The Last Farewell'. Returning to Mackay, he had played keys for Steve Harley & Cockney Rebel, 10cc and then Kate Bush on her first three LPs, so he was a great fit. Ward and Bass, of course, remained the rhythm section.

In addition to the core band, Mel Collins re-joined in the studio accompanied by the handful of minor contributors listed above.

The accompanying Europe-only tour was a sell-out, spanning January to April 1981, ending with a second 'by popular demand' appearance at the Hammersmith Odeon.

Apart from the Hammond work – which is all Mackay – and Schelhaas' named contribution on 'The Last Farewell', due to Latimer's keyboard credit, it's hard to unpick exactly who is playing what on the album. So without access to the studio logs, unless the player is obvious, I'm not going to speculate.

One final observation: it's notable that Latimer doesn't at any stage in the composition stray into any Japanese musical tropes, and for this, he is to be applauded. It would have been easy to overdo the koto or to include some wadaiko drums or nokhan flutes, but instead, he lets the story stand on its own. *Nude* is a better work for it.

'City Life' (Latimer, Hoover)

Japan is at war, and the twenty-year-old Nude is living in Tokyo but not yet called up. He muses over the direction his nation is taking and hankers after the past, when the country had more traditional values.

Starting off with a sort of 'reverse lullaby' comprising Bass's fretless bass over synth arpeggios, the vocals soon arrive and then the pace changes as Ward joins in with a steady driving beat mirrored by some chirpy electric piano, the effect nicely calling to mind someone waking up and hearing the bustle of the city outside. Over a couple of verses, Bass and Latimer seamlessly share the singing duties and sound great together (you can hear Bass's slight lisp at times, which is a stamp of authenticity for his parts).

The bridge brings another change of tempo with a fun tambourine and drum exchange between left and right channels, leading into a classic Collins sax break, one more sung verse, and ending with a restrained solo from Latimer that's unusually far back in the mix. We're up and running, all systems 'Go'.

'Nude' (Latimer)

At 23 seconds long, this is the shortest track in the Camel catalogue. Apart from that claim to infamy, there's not much more to say: 'Nude' should properly be regarded as simply an outro to 'City Life', comprising as it does, nothing but some distorted synth, and logically should have been tacked on to that track. Puzzling.

'Drafted' (Latimer, Hoover)

Nude is called up for service. The opening theme, a minor key duet by Mackay on piano and Chris Green's languid cello, is suitably melancholic, suggesting bad news on the way. Hoover's lyrics show that Nude has reservations, but as a loyal citizen, in the end, he has no choice but to accept his fate, and as such, 'Drafted' is the most personal character study of our protagonist.

The first verse leads into a trademark clean, melodic Latimer guitar solo, then a change of pace with a jaunty middle section before the second verse and some glorious full-band harmonisations. Lavish arrangement and Latimer's slide guitar in the endpiece somehow reminds me of ELO, which is a compliment, I promise.

'Docks' (Latimer, Watkins)

Nude is on his way to war, mustering at the docks before getting on deck for his fateful journey southwest.

Remember my critique of 'Eye of the Storm' on *I Can See Your House from Here*? Although Watkins doesn't play on *Nude*, he's credited as co-writer of 'Docks', which adds credence to my theory that they were already working on the music for the next album while at the Farmyard, yet not at that stage having a firm concept in place.

'Docks', and next track 'Beached', also call back to 'Preparation' and 'Dunkirk' on *Snow Goose*, which isn't surprising given the context of boarding a ship and the wartime backdrop. It's an interesting and illuminating exercise to play these four tracks back-to-back.

Latimer's string-bending, tremolo arm pushing and heavily reverbed Gilmour-influenced playing is the highlight of the first section, which is followed by a short cinematic bridge, that implies the ship sailing away, the effect enhanced by some portentous de-tuned piano chords. Then we're back to a short reprise of the first theme before segueing into …

'Beached' (Latimer)

… the epic double-time blast of 'Beached': let battle commence. The heavily syncopated music brilliantly evokes the stuttering ups and downs, two steps forward, one step back rhythm of an amphibious assault, with a short brass interlude suggesting a successful landing, only to be followed by a push back into the sea, before finally gaining a beachhead represented by a modulation in the major. As with most of *Nude*, this is another Latimer soloing showcase, backed by a band in full swing and having a whale of a time.

Due to its overall composition, changes of pace and dynamics, storytelling and musicianship from all members, 'Beached' for me, this is by far the best track on the record, bringing act one of *Nude* to a stunning close.

'Landscapes' (Latimer)

Act two. For the purposes of Hoover's interpretation of the story, *Nude* is now alone on the island, abandoned by his unit. An ethereal flute solo floating above an ambient keyboard accompaniment suggests palm trees waving in the sea breeze, distant horizons and loneliness. 'Landscapes' captures the scene just about perfectly; it's a lovely interlude.

'Changing Places' (Latimer)

Tribal rhythms and a droning – almost like a didgeridoo – undercurrent capture the idea of Nude patrolling the jungle in his search for food and the enemy. Woodwind flourishes act as the calls of forest creatures hidden high in the canopy.

'Pomp & Circumstance' (Latimer)
The music is solemn in keeping with the mood, as Nude walks to the mountain top to contemplate his situation and fulfil his duty by firing off a salutary shot in honour of the 'East Asian Co-Prosperity Zone', or the Japanese Empire, as the rest of the world referred to it.

I should probably duck for cover, but does anyone else hear just a little hint of Vangelis here? Then there's Ward with his martial snare drum rolls again, and we hear the shot into the air. A poignant moment in the narrative.

'Please Come Home' (Latimer)
Although this passage is important to the story, 'Please Come Home' doesn't really *hit* home. Musically it's all a bit twee and viewed in isolation, it's the weakest 73 seconds on the album. To recap: leaflets are being dropped on the island saying that the war is over, but Onoda thinks this is propaganda and so, for the moment at least, he ignores them.

'Reflections' (Latimer, Schelhaas)
Schelhaas gets a writing credit here, so again I'm inclined to think that this was born during the time at The Farmyard and not during the *Nude* sessions where the keyboard player joined for 'The Last Farewell' only.

Airy synths and trademark Latimer guitar paint a scene of tranquillity and deep thought, reflection indeed. As the sleeve notes recount:

> In the days that followed, Nude was no longer at one with his environment ... burdened with the need to explain the inexplicable.

This tender musical passage gives nothing away about what happens next, so the shock value of what's coming is utterly concealed.

'Captured' (Latimer)
Andy Latimer deploys the koto in style, but not in a traditional tuning, I might add, and it's the one and only direct reference to Japanese music on the whole album. The koto, of course, represents the incoming Japanese 'rescue squad', and when that posse does arrive, the music comes in with a bang. The frantic pace is certainly evocative, but at times it feels overdone and one does occasionally get the impression of a fast-forward Benny Hill-style chase around the beach. Nevertheless, 'Captured' is an example of terrific ensemble playing, having no solos as such, which suits the subject matter really well, with Latimer's recurring descending acoustic guitar riff something, in particular, to listen out for.

End of act two.

'The Homecoming' (Latimer)
Nude is back in Japan, but it doesn't feel like home. Herbie Flowers, of T-Rex and Sky fame, joins in on tuba, but although his oompah-ing is appropriate to the scene, he isn't exactly stretched by the score as the marching band, with its massed flutes, pans from left to right. 'Homecoming' is important as part of the *Nude* story, less so as a piece of music. Ward is at his military snare drum again; was he trying to tell us something with his penchant for paradiddling?

'Lies' (Latimer, Hoover)
Everything we've heard since 'City Life' could reasonably be categorised as 'mood music', so 'Lies' is the first proper song since then. It's a laid-back and bluesy number enhanced by Latimer initially channelling Mark Knopfler in style and in both meanings of that word.

Mackay delivers a tremendous Hammond solo, the first significant showcase for that instrument since the Bardens days before Latimer presents us with a brilliantly executed blues solo straight out of Ry Cooder's top drawer. The versatility of the man is outstanding.

'The Last Farewell: The Birthday Cake' (Latimer)
More artistic licence taken here with the plot, as at no time during Onoda's return was he confined to a hospital for months. Anyway, the nurses at the facility present him with a 50th birthday cake shaped and decorated like a tropical island. You'd have thought that after 30 years as a castaway, the last thing he'd want to be reminded of is a deserted lagoon in the middle of nowhere, but it is what it is.

That observation aside, 'The Birthday Cake' lasts only 30 seconds before invisibly melding into 'Nude's Return'.

'The Last Farewell: Nude's Return' (Latimer)
At this point, Camel's narrative departs completely from history. According to contemporary reports, Onoda was unhappy in the media spotlight and perturbed by what he saw as the gradual erosion of traditional Japanese values.

Far from retreating to the island that had been his enforced home for 30 years, as inferred by the song title and spelt out in the sleeve notes, in 1975, he followed his elder brother Tadao and left Japan for Brazil, where he raised cattle. Marrying in 1976, he assumed a leading role in the Japanese community in Terenos.

Post the period covered by *Nude*, which, remember, was recorded in 1981, upon reading in 1984 about a teenager who had in 1980 murdered his parents after failing his exams, Onoda returned to Japan and established the Onoda Nature School. This is a multi-location foundation to help young people understand more about ecology, natural philosophy and living off the land, thus hopefully mitigating any nascent destructive tendencies that he believed were latent in the younger generation of Japanese. Onoda died in Tokyo in 2014, at the ripe old age of 92.

Nevertheless, 'Nude's Return' is a fitting musical conclusion to the tale, cinematic in conception and containing all the elements we love: a classic melodic solo from Latimer that continues pretty much through the whole song, Ward's judicious fills and military snare rolls, Bass harmonising on the bass, and all fading out into the metaphorical distance. Yes: *Nude* really is a return to form.

Above: Kit Watkins during the notorious mimed performance of 'City Life' on BBC's *Old Grey Whistle Test* in 1981. A be-bereted and taking it less-than-seriously Andy Ward is in the background. (*BBC*)

Left: A fresh-faced Mr Bass 'singing' 'City Life' on the BBC's *Old Grey Whistle* Test in 1981: the eyebrows are yet to attain their future magnificence. (*BBC*)

The Single Factor (1982)

Personnel:

Andy Latimer: lead vocals, guitar, piano, keyboards, Mellotron ('Manic'), organ ('Today's Goodbye'), bass ('Manic')

David Paton: bass, backing vocals, lead vocals ('Heroes')

Chris Rainbow: backing vocals, lead vocals ('A Heart's Desire')

Anthony Phillips: organ ('Heroes', 'Manic'), grand piano ('Heroes', 'Manic', 'End Peace'), Polymoog ('Manic, End Peace'), ARP 2600 ('End Peace'), marimba ('End Peace'), acoustic guitar ('Selva'), 12-string guitar ('Sasquatch')

Graham Jarvis: drums, percussion

Additional musicians

Peter Bardens: organ, Minimoog ('Sasquatch')

Haydn Bendall: Yamaha CS80 synthesizer ('Heroes')

Duncan Mackay: Prophet synthesizer ('Selva')

Francis Monkman: Synclavier ('Manic')

Dave Mattacks: drums, percussion ('Heroes')

Simon Phillips: drums, percussion ('Sasquatch')

Tristan Fry: glockenspiel ('Manic')

Jack Emblow: accordion ('A Heart's Desire')

Produced by Tony Clarke, Andy Latimer and Haydn Bendall at Abbey Road, Studio 3, London, Jan/Feb 1982

Engineer: Tony Clarke

Release date: 6 May 1982

Running time: 39:01

Current edition: Esoteric Recordings ECLEC 2156

Highest chart places: UK: 57

At this stage in Camel's life, although desperate for an extended break for reasons we're about to come to, Latimer was getting increasingly pressurised by Decca to write a hit single or three, and there was also the contractual obligation to deliver an album in 1982. After all, what the label saw was that in the previous year, progressive rock had renewed momentum and was gradually returning to vogue after the punk years. Genesis had released *Abacab* and Rush brought *Moving Pictures* into the world, so 'Look how those did, Andy'.

Mr. Latimer's riposte was this album, considered by many critics and fans alike to be the low point of a generally illustrious career. There's nothing bad *per se* with any of the tracks, but trying to be both objective and frank, it is a mishmash of styles, all of which hover like a gadfly in the region of the classic Camel sound but never settle into that special Camel groove. Of course, as history proved, none of the eleven numbers would result in that elusive hit single.

You can tell through the music that Latimer was fed up with the pressure from the label management and A&R people, so calling the album *The Single Factor* was probably the least career-damaging way to let off steam. Of course,

Latimer was effectively the only bona fide Camel member left in the room. Bass was off on his travels, leaving the *Nude* tour bus in Paris and staying for six months to collaborate on an album with jazz saxophonist Jim Cuomo, and as for Andy Ward, well, it's time to tell that story.

Over the years, Ward had become more and more erratic, drinking heavily and prone to extreme mood swings. This reached its zenith, or nadir, depending on your perspective, during the *Nude* tour. At the time, Bass and Ward – who had become close friends – were sharing a flat in Notting Hill, and the end of that tour coincided with the end of the lease on the apartment, sending them their separate ways.

Exactly what happened next is privileged information, but suffice to say that Ward attempted suicide by cutting his wrist, ending up in a psychiatric unit for five months to be medicated, counselled and start on his road to recovery. Ultimately, he was diagnosed with bipolar disorder, and suddenly his behaviour made sense. In Ward's own words: 'I didn't so much leave Camel, than fall off ...'.

Members of the band freely admit that they hadn't realised the extent of Ward's problems and the penny hadn't dropped that he was, in actuality, seriously ill. Thankfully, now aware of his condition, Ward recuperated extremely well, but although remaining close friends with the rest of the band, never again played for Camel. *The Single Factor* sleeve notes diplomatically stated, 'Andy Ward did not appear on this album following a serious injury to his hand'.

On *CV*, Latimer says of the time:

> When Andy left, I didn't really want to carry on. I didn't see any point in continuing as Camel, it took me two years to get over his leaving. It was a very hard album to do. I was basically coerced and sweet-talked into doing it. You could tell that I was hurting and directionless: Camel was probably at its lowest point.

Other personnel changes further complicated matters ahead of the sessions: Jan Schelhaas is on record stating he needed a break as his son had just been born, and if he was going to continue touring, he would miss him growing up. Under these circumstances, he bravely took the opportunity to enrol as a mature student and read a combined Music and Philosophy degree at Middlesex Polytechnic (now University), telling Mark Powell in 2008:

> I was glad that I did because it helped me understand some compositional techniques that I may have known instinctively but never formalised. It enabled me to do orchestrations which I couldn't do before.

As Kit Watkins had also left the fold with his Camel ambitions unrealised, Latimer stood alone as the only original, or indeed fully-ordained, band member and so assembled a group of friends and session players to join him at Abbey Road.

Although you wouldn't guess it from first listen, Ant Phillips of early Genesis fame is a major contributor, playing on five of the eleven tracks and co-writing one. Ant became involved as a result of a growing friendship with Latimer, who lived nearby Phillips' Clapham house, and his quasi-classical stylings are clear and present on the tracks he's involved with, with the 12-string Rickenbacker opening riff on 'Sasquatch' straight out of the Genesis Family Playbook. A lovely anecdote that Ant shared with me was that he and Latimer had been carol singing in Chelsea the previous Christmas, and unsurprisingly given the average denizen of that postcode, their stature as musicians went unremarked and they received a less than resounding response. So, it's clear that they were close.

Around this time, Andy L and Ant P (through his connections in the film music industry) were approached to write the score for *The Terminator*, with the script doing the rounds in London at that time. This job ended up with Brad Friedel, and the rest is history. The only jointly-penned 'soundtrack' from this Latimer-Phillips collaboration that saw the light of day was music for a Land Rover TV advertisement that also got used as incidental music for the European PGA Golf Tour. Just imagine what might have happened to Latimer's career if they had got the gig for *The Terminator* instead.

Apart from the commercial pressure, more direct interference in the studio was also a sticking point, with Max Hole's then-partner at one point piping up with 'That's so wimpy' during the recording of a Latimer-Phillips penned neo-classical piece that ended up on the cutting room floor. This prompted one of the storied duo's many strolls along the Abbey Road corridors to the cavernous and almost mythical Studio Two for decompression and a spirited game of frisbee using snare drumheads.

Then there's the Alan Parsons Project connection: the band were at Abbey Road recording the ultimately Grammy Award-winning *Eye in the Sky*, which on first release, peaked at number seven in the US *Billboard* Charts and number 27 in the UK, and at time of writing, has sold in excess of two million copies worldwide. You might say it was a hit. David Paton had met Latimer at Abbey Road when Camel were recording the *Nude* sessions and stayed in touch. So it was that Paton and fellow APP-er, vocalist Chris Rainbow joined the gang.

In addition to Ant Phillips and the Alan Parsons Project guys, *Single Factor*'s Cecil B. DeMille-like cast of thousands included three (count 'em, three) drummers: Cliff Richard's go-to session man Graham Jarvis, Dave Mattacks from Fairport Convention and technical stick-holding virtuoso, *Modern Drummer* magazine Hall of Famer Simon Phillips. Rounding off the roll call, Sky were also at Abbey Road, adding the finishing touches to *Sky 4*, so Tristan Fry chipped in as well, as did friend and ex-Sky (and Curved Air) keysman Francis Monkman. Last but not least, accordion player Jack Emblow squeezed his box on 'A Heart's Desire': it has to be said that you pretty much need a spreadsheet with pivot tables to understand who did what and when.

One final welcome bonus to the line-up is, of course, Peter Bardens, who adds his special touch to the barnstorming live favourite, 'Sasquatch', sadly his final studio contribution to Camel's oeuvre.

Camel toured *The Single Factor* from May to September 1982, in Europe only. On stage, the personnel comprised Latimer, Watkins (again returning to tour but not present on the album) plus Andy Dalby from Arthur Brown's Kingdom Come on second guitar, David Paton on bass, Chris Rainbow on keyboards and vocals, and The Alan Parsons Project's Stuart Tosh on drums. Having three Scotsmen with him on the road, Latimer remembers the road fondly as 'the funniest tour I've ever been on'.

Onto the music ...

'No Easy Answer' (Latimer)

Trying to be overtly radio-friendly, sub-three minute 'No Easy Answer' is a foretaste of things to come on this LP. It's a forgettable, upbeat pop song more suited to the 70s than the 80s – think The Carpenters, what with all the 'la la la' stuff, but without that duo's depth. Of course, the precision production – as you might expect from Abbey Road – is top-notch, as is the playing, including a 12-string jangling in the background and Latimer's chorused solo outro, but this doesn't save what in the end is no better than average FM fodder.

'You Are The One' (Latimer)

Released as the only 45 from *The Single Factor*, sadly, it's no great surprise that this didn't chart when the competition at the time included 'House of Fun' by Madness, 'Only You' by Yazoo and 'The Look of Love' by ABC. What was the record label thinking? Oh, yes, they wanted a hit record.

Doing my best to be generous to my favourite band of all time, this slice of AOR pop-rock does have its moments: the boppy chorus is a real singalong, multiple keyboards add depth to the production, and Latimer's power riffing and pick slides – sparse though they may be – is at the heavier end of his stylistic spectrum, and great to hear. Ultimately, 'You Are the One' didn't find its way onto many Camel mix-tapes, and for good reason.

'Heroes' (Latimer, Hoover)

Very, very Alan Parsons Project. It's not only David Paton's vocals, but it's the production and instrumentation as well, that mark it out as the one that got away in the APP catalogue.

Ant Phillips at the grand piano, accompanied by Haydn Bendall on the seminal Yamaha CS80 synth, get us on the way with somewhat muted fanfare. Paton's voice is instantly recognisable, singing about images, idols and nameless heroes; some depth and complexity are introduced by sequencer arpeggiations that skitter up and down behind the vocals.

Heroes is the first song on the album involving Susan Hoover's lyrics, and as we'll discover later on, her talents in this department matured dramatically over subsequent albums. Lines like 'Make me secure – be my fallacy' show a wordsmith still taking only their first tentative steps on the road to bard-dom.

In another setting, the power ballad chorus might have worked well, but here paradoxically, it seems somehow under-blown – some brass and strings might have made the difference, but far be it for me to suggest tinkering with Clarke and Bendall's unquestionable production and arranging abilities.

So, it's harmless enough, but it ain't Camel, folks. Latimer is all but invisible – only a few bars of acoustic guitar are front and centre in the mix – and given those call and response vocals that play us out, did I mention that this is basically an Alan Parsons Project song?

'Selva' (Latimer)

There's no question that 'Selva' is a beautiful piece of music, with Latimer's soloing soaring above Ant Phillips' melodic nylon-strung classical guitar and Mackay's atmospheric chords on the Prophet 5. Compared to the rest of *Single Factor*, it is more in keeping with the early Camel feel – the Latimer bluesy soloing sees to that – but even so, it's missing something intangible, something that marks it out as real Camel. As a section of a lengthier piece from the band, I think we'd see this passage in a totally different light, appended, for example, to 'Elke' to produce something akin to a classical rhapsody. As such, 'Selva' is a missed opportunity.

'Lullabye' (Latimer)

Latimer sits down at the piano and sings a sub-one-minute lullaby in the style of Randy Newman or, at a stretch, Billy Joel. It's pretty enough and his lyrics are clearly heartfelt, but like 'Heroes', this just isn't Camel. There's nothing wrong with the compact ditty *per se*, but as a side closer, the choice is baffling. Last track on side two? Sure – why not – but the placement here is just wrong, although those who never had the LP and just the CD will probably never have cottoned on to the incongruity.

Under the circumstances, many fans therefore, couldn't be bothered to immediately turn the record over, which, as we will now see, was a grave error in the context of the album as a whole.

'Sasquatch' (Latimer)

Fans who had been with Camel from the early days may be forgiven for giving up by this stage, consigning the LP to the 'maybe again later' pile, but that would have been a monstrously big boo-boo. It's time to wind up the amp, people, as 'Sasquatch' rocks. And that 12-string intro? No less than original Genesis strummer Ant Phillips. This one's so riff-laden that it's amazing it doesn't explode under the internal pressure.

Simon Phillips' seriously intricate drum work? Check. Latimer wigging out like a champ, pick scratching and all? Check. Bardens' heavenly Hammond and Minimoog playing? Check. And, of course, Dave Paton steering the whole thing along with metronomic precision.

Going back to the drum work, a little bird told me – and I'm not going to name names – that the touring drummers had a hard time trying to unpick Simon Phillips' chops. It's no wonder that he's still in demand, appearing most recently on ex-Dream Theater keysman Derek Sherinian's 2020 LP, *The Phoenix*, which he also produced.

'Sasquatch' is the only bona fide Camel classic on the album. Does the song have anything to do with the legendary Bigfoot? Err, yes and no: according to Susan Hoover, it's about Andy Latimer's huge feet – but who cares what it's about as it's a foot-stomping, arms-in-the-air, good times tune and a regular feature of the live set – so that's good enough for me.

'Manic' (Latimer, Hoover)
'Manic' it certainly is, if dictionary definitions are anything to go by: 'wild, apparently deranged, excitement and energy, frantically busy, hectic'. They threw the kitchen sink, as well as the fridge, cooker, microwave and dining table, at this one. Whisper it softly, but given the time and circumstances, one might logically draw the conclusion that the lyrics refer to a certain recently ex-member of the band, but the case has never (officially) been proven, and I'm not going to go there.

Adding to the confusion, it's so damn over-produced – and as we found out with 'Neon Magic' on *I Can See Your House From Here*, the laconic Mr. Latimer doesn't do attitude well, with his angry vocal delivery unconvincing at best, although maybe this time the emotion is genuine given the painful subject matter. Doing my best to be charitable, Latimer certainly throws some heavy and accomplished licks into the mix, but it's not enough to save the song.

Topping it off, Tristan Fry's glockenspiel seems particularly superfluous to the compositional cocktail (I can just imagine the conversation in the Abbey Road canteen 'Is that a glockenspiel, Tristan?' 'Yes' 'OK: why the devil not – you're in') and the end-section is another APP influenced effect-fest with the whole clock chiming and de-tuned church organ patch on the synth thing. Finally, the outro, complete with dystopian intervals and an ambient fade out, is probably meant to suggest the medication is kicking in.

For some reason, the scattergun approach of 'Manic' always reminds me of Sparks' 'This Town Ain't Big Enough For Both Of Us', so 'Manic' is about as far away as you can get from the Camel we know and love, but I suppose at least it's different.

'Camelogue' (Latimer, Hoover)
It's not only the use of 'crosswalk' that makes this a very American-sounding number. Latimer's competent bluesy guitar isn't enough to rescue 'Camelogue', a mid-tempo AOR offering of the Foreigner ilk. It also has too many wordless backing vocal interjections for my liking – always something that sets my teeth on edge.

On the plus side, the plodding, camel walking beat would be used to great effect many years later on *Rajaz*, so it's good to see that germinating here.

Subject-wise, Camelogue is undoubtedly autobiographical, detailing Latimer's then state of mind. With Ward gone, should he call it day or carry on with the band? Should he listen to the 'small talk' in the industry that was insinuating that his style of music was a goner.

Thankfully and luckily for all of us, he did, in fact, 'keep going for the song and the road'.

'Today's Goodbye' (Latimer, Hoover)
10cc, The Beach Boys or The Bee Gees? You decide. This is another clear attempt to get radio play and even though Latimer plays some cool jangly licks and slides, at the end of the day, 'Today's Goodbye' is just a cookie-cutter pop song released into a world already full to the brim with cookie-cutter pop songs. All the 'oohing' and 'ahh-ing' merely adds to the genericity and as fans, we must all, to a greater or lesser extent, feel empathy for the conflict that Latimer was experiencing at that time – on this showing, his heart simply wasn't in it.

'A Heart's Desire' (Latimer, Hoover)
On the subject of hearts, this is another APP side dish, and at only a minute and change in length, it's hard to find a cogent argument for its inclusion. I suppose it's pretty enough, but it smacks of an offcut that could have been included in any number of places elsewhere in either Camel's or The Alan Parsons Project's output. Jack Emblow's accordion is a pleasant addition, giving a sort of Parisian street-side café feel to things – but is this really Camel we're hearing? 'A Heart's Desire' seamlessly melds into ...

'End Peace' (Latimer, Phillips)
Like some of the earlier cuts on *The Single Factor*, 'End Peace' sounds too much like leftovers. Two of progressive rock's most brilliant lights, Andy Latimer and Ant Phillips, undeniably deliver an atmospheric bookend for the album, and the understated playing is gorgeous, but why here and on this album? Phillips had the right idea when he gathered together his bits and bobs and released them as the *Private Parts & Pieces* LPs. After this, the pair drifted apart, but there's still time for another collaboration, surely?

Stationary Traveller (1984)

Personnel:
Andrew Latimer: guitars, vocals, bass, synthesizers, piano, drum synthesiser, flute, Pan pipes.
Ton Scherpenzeel: keyboards and accordion
Paul Burgess: drums, percussion
Additional musicians
David Paton: bass
Chris Rainbow: vocals
Mel Collins: saxophone
Haydn Bendall: Fairlight and PPG synths
Produced by Andy Latimer at Riverside Studios, England, then mixed in Los Angeles, California and mastered at The Mastering Lab, Los Angeles
Engineer: Dave Hutchins
Release date: 13 April 1984
Running time: 42:14 (original) 48:36 (2009 re-release)
Current edition: Esoteric Records ECLEC 2154
Highest Chart Places: UK: 57

On the back of the new fans that *Rain Dances* and *Breathless* had brought into the fold, it's inevitable that *The Single Factor* was going to chart, which it indeed did but not breaking the Top 50 in the UK and missing out altogether in the USA. Nevertheless, with the original contract now almost discharged, Decca committed to one more album.

Personnel-wise, once more Dave Paton put his hand up for the bass seat, and Alan Parsons Project teammate, Chris Rainbow, again signed on for vocals. New to the band, ex-10cc and Jethro Tull man Paul Burgess took on drum duty and Kayak founder Dutchman Ton Scherpenzeel brought his symphonic flair behind the keyboards, ably supported by Haydn Bendall on synths. Rounding out the roster, Camel alumnus Mel Collins chipped in on one track, 'Fingertips'. No spreadsheet needed this time, then. Bass was still on his travels but would return for the tour – brilliantly captured on the *Pressure Points CD* and DVD.

Another album, and yet another studio – this time Riverside Studios in Hammersmith, London. Although Soft Machine had recorded *Land Of Cockayne* there a few years prior to the *Stationary Traveller* sessions, it needs to be remarked that the facility was better known as a TV and movie filming venue than for music production. Abbey Road it was not, with Decca obviously deciding that the final record of the deal didn't merit such largesse.

Stationary Traveller is not a concept album as such but does have an overall theme, conceived by Susan Hoover: life in Berlin during the Cold War. Each of the tracks takes on a separate theme or personal perspective, from the building of the Berlin Wall in 1961 to a would-be asylum seeker eventually making it to the West. The album is a work of its time – remember that in 1984, the Wall was still in place, and it was not until the end of 1989 that it was breached.

In this writer's opinion *Stationary Traveller*, even given the title track, is the weakest of the fourteen studio albums – even more so than *The Single Factor*, which is saved by 'Sasquatch' and, to a lesser extent, 'Selva'. Thankfully, though, it represents the end of another era for the band and gives no indication of the torrent of creative energy that would be forthcoming as a result of Latimer and Hoover's decision to both emigrate and go it alone.

'Pressure Points' (Latimer)
From its Nine Inch Nails-style industrial synth intro to the guitar tapping close, 'Pressure Points' indicates that this time we're in for something quite different from Latimer & Co. This is underlined by his squealing main melody that commences in the opening bars and continues throughout, in true guitar hero fashion.

Bendall ground those heavyweight synthesiser noises and 'Owner Of A Lonely Heart' orchestral crashes out of Kate Bush's Fairlight Series Two. The Fairlight Series was the first-ever 'sampling' synth, which sold for a 2021-inflation-adjusted £106,000 when introduced in 1982 – you could probably have bought a Stradivarius for less than that back then.

Brits of a certain age may remember a somewhat over-excited Kieran Prendiville demonstrating the instrument on the BBC's *Tomorrow's World*, and if your memory doesn't extend that far back, or you're from a country that never had the pleasure of the programme, seek it out on one of the popular 'tube' sites – it's a gem. Nonetheless, the beast sounds great and, as an element of the overture to the coming subject matter, it's an appropriate use of cutting-edge tech.

'Refugee' (Latimer, Hoover)
It's a bit of a surprise to hear the Supertramp-ish, pop-prog, electric piano-led bounciness of 'Refugee' as the next track: what happened to all the heaviness we were promised mere seconds ago?

Latimer sings Hoover's lyrics about an East Berliner watching the building of the Berlin Wall, which, let's face it, must have been a seriously harrowing experience, so the jauntiness of the music is a little jarring. Putting the mood of the track to one side, the guitarist's finger-style licks are a joy to hear and his voice never sounded better.

With its catchy singalong chorus, in other hands – and vocal cords – this could well have been a hit, especially with Scherpenzeel's heavily-processed accordion – believe it or not, that's a thing, apparently – providing some interesting atmosphere in the background. Ultimately though, I feel that the music just doesn't do justice to the seriousness of the subject matter.

'Vopos' (Latimer, Hoover)
The 'Vopos' were the East German Volkspolizei – the national police force of the GDR that expanded over time to incorporate the dreaded Stasi, and unlike

'Refugee' this time the threatening mood and spooky music are bang on for the lyrical content.

Once again, we hear the Fairlight in all its glory, part of an ensemble of six synths and a Drumulator. Once it gets going after the atmospheric intro, no wonder this number sounds like Kraftwerk (if I'm going to be kind) or Depeche Mode in all their pomp (if I'm not). Latimer just about manages to temper the synth-pop with some power chords and bluesy solo work, which goes some way to relieving the tedium, elevating it above the more mundane offerings of said genre.

'Cloak And Dagger Man' (Latimer, Hoover)

Chris Rainbow joins on vocals, which once more, somewhat inevitably, turns a Latimer song into an Alan Parsons Project project. As has been discussed in earlier chapters, Latimer, Bardens, Ferguson and Bass's voices – although not in any way the greatest of vocal talents – give Camel a crucial element of the band's trademark sound, so lovely as Rainbow's voice is, it can't help but water down the Camel-ness of the piece.

As should be obvious from the title, the lyrics refer to the surveillance state that was so terrible a factor of living in East Germany, and East Berlin in particular, during the years of the Cold War. 'Checking all around' and keeping one's head down while watching out for sundry cross-dressers, and the stark message that even those closest to you will inform on any perceived 'unpatriotic' behaviour.

Music-wise, the jittery synth riff provides the element of suspense, interspersed with an occasional power chord from Latimer, whose short solos seem a little lost in the fog. Scherpenzeel, who in his Camel position was more used to playing an orchestral, chord-based supporting role, shows us that he shines in solos too, delivering a cracking passage on a Juno 60, calling to mind a chase through dark alleyways in almost parkour style.

'Stationary Traveller' (Latimer)

And now, we have the one true Camel masterpiece on *Stationary Traveller* and it's a stunner. At last, on the album, we have a multiple passage composition of the old Camel school. The completely left-field combination of pan pipes and a synth programmed to sound like a hammered dulcimer is pure magic. Latimer's emotional solo is outstanding – not quite *Ice* outstanding, but certainly one for the trophy cabinet. Vitally, 'Stationary Traveller' has *momentum:* although down-tempo, it drives forward with purpose and what might have ended up as a dirge in actuality becomes an uplifting anthem of hope.

'Stationary Traveller', of course, refers to the people stuck on the GDR side of the Berlin Wall, unable to get there physically but dreaming of escape to the West: the wistful, dreamy quality of the music evokes this state of mind really well. It's a regular feature of live sets, deservedly so.

'West Berlin' (Latimer, Hoover)

Very much in the vein of 'Refugee', but this time more *Love Over Gold*-era Dire Straits than Supertramp, the song's protagonist is an East Berliner staring at the freedom that beckons in West Berlin, knowing that in all likelihood it would be a one-way journey. With Latimer behind the mic, it qualifies as a proper Camel number, which is a relief, and in another setting, the catchy chorus would have been right at home if found in any number of 80s hit singles.

That dulcimer riff is pinched directly from any number of Cold War spy movies, which is a cute touch and Scherpenzeel shines again with his measured synth soloing in the outro.

'Fingertips' (Latimer, Hoover)

You might think from the overall mood of 'Fingertips' that this is a love song about leaving someone behind, but, in fact, it's an ode to the place the narrator is about to leave as he makes for the West. It's the chance to defect that might slip through those fingertips, not romantic love.

Vocally, 'Fingertips' has one of Latimer's most accomplished performances, using his full range and showing us some real emotion. It's also nice to hear the mellow sax tones of Mel Collins for the one and only time on *Stationary Traveller*. A judicious selection of fretless bass rounds off the tender sound.

'Missing' (Latimer)

Our hero is making his midnight flit to the West. Missing tells the story by using furtive keyboard figures and heavy syncopation in 7/8 that suggest peeking round corners and scuttling from dark alley to dark alley, avoiding the searchlights and secret police (in drag or otherwise), represented again by the dulcimer. If the album has a showcase for Latimer's guitar, then this is it; he deploys a variety of pedals to great effect.

'After Words' (Scherpenzeel)

Pretty vignette, 'After Words', has Scherpenzeel once more on grand piano and accordion, is another of those Camel mini tracks that seem to have been included on an album to fill space rather than be saved for another time to be worked into a more complete offering. However, all is not as it seems. The accordion is actually the 'harmonium' preset on a Prophet 5 and is frankly indistinguishable from the real thing. So, on 'Refugee', he uses an accordion like a synth, and on 'After Words', he uses a synth as an accordion. If this was a deliberate musical joke on the Dutchman's part, it's brilliant.

As a follow-up to 'Missing', the number's melancholy and regretful tone nevertheless evokes relief, safety and hope for the future. Any hi-jinks, intentionally or otherwise from the keyboard player, don't detract from the beautiful counterpoint between the piano and 'accordion', I just wish this had been extended into something longer and substantial.

'Long Goodbyes' (Latimer, Hoover)

Finally, on *Stationary Traveller* we have Latimer's adorable flute chirruping over a repeating acoustic guitar figure. Are we about to hear some proper Camel? Sadly, no. I'm not going to point out the obvious, but Chris Rainbow's vocals – luscious though they are – infuriatingly turn this into a track that would be more suited to his 'other' band's output, indeed something the singer himself once observed, as quoted earlier. The lilting tune and lavish orchestrations from the synths only add to the feeling that, as Camel fans, we're being a tad short-changed.

Nonetheless, Latimer's unquestionable melodic songwriting ability, as well as his lovely solo – heavily compressed in the effects and a favourite of many, saves the day. Live as a set closer on recent tours – sans Rainbow – the number has found a new lease of life.

Maybe not only due to the subject matter but also because of the musical similarity to a certain man's 'Project', 'Long Goodbyes' was released in Germany as a single on the local Metronome label – part of the Polygram group; 'In The Arms Of Waltzing Frauleins' was the B-side (more about that track below).

Associated tracks
'In The Arms Of Waltzing Frauleins' (Latimer, Hoover)

It's difficult to find a cogent argument as to why this track was left off the original release. Considering the concept of the album, it perfectly sets the scene with Chris Rainbow making a reasonable stab at Marlene Dietrich-esque delivery without hamming it and more of that accordion. I particularly like the use of massed male voices as a backing, evoking as it does a communist-era choir, so amplifying the atmosphere.

On the out-of-print 2004 Camel Productions release, it sits as track one, but on the 2009 Cherry Red release, it's tacked on to the end as bonus material. My personal preference is with the 2004 ordering. 'In The Arms ...' also tops and tails the original *Pressure Points Live In Concert* VHS/DVD, but not the expanded *Total Pressure* DVD release from 2006.

'Pressure Points' – 12" version (Latimer)

The Eighties was the decade of the venerable 12" single, with tracks like Ultravox's 'Vienna' selling by the cartload in this format. So it was that in Decca's wisdom 'Cloak And Dagger Man' was also released as a 12" for no better reason than to edit a triple-length extended mix of 'Pressure Points' and use that to pad out the available space on the B-side (the A-side track was unedited from the 7" version).

The first two minutes are indistinguishable from the album track: a short ambient section follows and then Latimer plays an atmospheric solo that, to be frank, is little more than a meditation on 'Shine On ...' by Floyd. Next up is some pretty noodling from keys and lead guitar before we get all Industrial again for the last minute.

One is left with the feeling that this was cobbled together with studio offcuts from the album sessions, and it serves no real purpose in the grand Camel scheme of things: on the plus side, at least Decca didn't insist on a club mix.

Above: Paul Burgess doing his stuff behind the kit on the *Stationary Traveller* tour at the Hammersmith Odeon in 1984. (*Camel Productions*)

Below: Dear departed Chris Rainbow on keys and vocals, again during the *Stationary Traveller* tour at the Hammersmith Odeon in 1984. (*Camel Productions*)

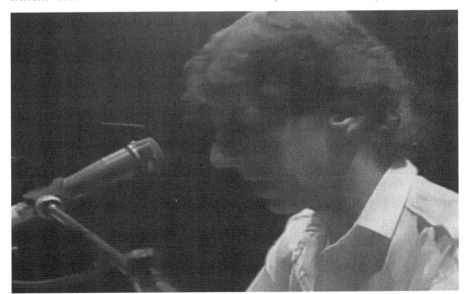

Interlude: The 'Lost' Years

During the creative hiatus after *Stationary Traveller*, Latimer was plagued with legal problems. Geoff Jukes sued Camel for past commissions and so Latimer, as the sole original member still performing in Camel, had to defend the lawsuit, on and off, for almost six years. If this wasn't stressful and distracting enough, Susan Hoover – by now de-facto manager of the band – had uncovered the shocking news that royalties from Camel's Decca back catalogue, although transferred from the record company to the management company (DJM), were not then being paid-on to the songwriters.

As a result of this revelation, Latimer had to countersue GAMA Records, still owned by Geoff Jukes and Max Hole. Latimer engaged the support of his former bandmates and, after finally settling their lawsuit with GAMA, received the first of many royalty payments to come. These formalities completed, the Timeline on Camel Productions' website happily informs us that:

> ...they celebrated at a local pub until closing time. Old wounds healed, memories flourished and, though they no longer had interest in playing together, all parted as friends.

Overall, though, apart from the legally binding commitment for GAMA to start paying royalties, Latimer and his compadrés had won only a Pyrrhic victory: although both cases were found in the band's favour, given legal fees, court costs and general expenses, they received no overall financial gain from their efforts: 'I had enough to buy a bistro meal ... for one' says Latimer.

And so, in 1988, and still without record company backing, Latimer and Hoover decided that the best solution to Camel's enforced furlough and their continued personal wellbeing was to sell their house in London, which due to the crazy property market in the UK's capital from the 70s into the 80s was worth a literal fortune, and on 27 July up sticks to the USA, specifically Northern California. Even after all the moving expenses, liquidating the property provided enough to eventually buy some land on the coast near Silicon Valley, south of San Francisco, and build a dream house and studio on-site. The weather was going to be better, too.

A final, particularly aggravating aspect of those years for Latimer and Hoover, considering the stress induced by the legal battles, is that pretty much every label, management company, publisher or rights owner that ever had skin in the game up until then, between 1985 and 1991 shamelessly released a 'greatest hits' collection. Four in total hit the shelves, while no new material was forthcoming from Camel. Needless to say, these albums are beyond the scope of this book.

Dust And Dreams (1991)

Personnel:
Andrew Latimer: guitar, flute, keyboards, vocals
Colin Bass: bass
Ton Scherpenzeel: keyboards
Paul Burgess: drums, percussion
Additional musicians
Don Harriss: keyboards
Christopher Bock: drums, percussion
Neil Panton: oboe
Kim Venaas: timpani, harmonica
John Burton: French horn
David Paton: vocals
Mae McKenna: vocals
Produced by Andy Latimer at Upstairs at Harry's / Downstairs at Harry's
Engineer: Andy Latimer
Release date: 10 September 1991
Running time: 47:57
Current edition: Camel Productions CP-001CD
Highest chart places: did not chart

The move to California, and the freedom from the shackles of a recording contract this brought, was clearly the tonic that Andy Latimer and Susan Hoover needed at that point in their lives – both personal and artistic. This quantum jump in their circumstances unleashed a period of creativity that hadn't been seen in the Camel universe since *Moonmadness*.

Dust And Dreams was conceived in 1985, by which time the deal with Decca for *Stationary Traveller* was over – happily without rancour, I might add. After doing the rounds with both major and independent labels, Latimer came up blank. At best, record executives accused Camel of being past it and that Latimer should rest safe in the knowledge that his 70s body of work would always stand as a monument to the influence and importance of the band. At worst, after the well-publicised legal wrangles, some labels came to the conclusion that they just didn't want the hassle. Latimer and Hoover, though, had different ideas.

Camel Productions was incorporated in 1990, and for the first time in his career, Latimer had complete creative freedom. There were no more contractually enforceable deadlines, no more interference from label management and A&R – or indeed, tobacco company executives and no pressure to deliver a hit single – all of this was gone for good.

It's received wisdom that Marillion were the first of the prog bands to go it alone, but Camel beat them to the punch by five years – although without the crowdfunding and web-based model that Marillion pioneered. With Camel, it was more of a traditional cottage industry, with regular newsletters

– *Nature of the Beast* – that had order forms for media and merch on the back page.

Recording in multiple locations in the days before the Internet was a complicated affair. Although the initial material for *Dust And Dreams* was recorded in London at Latimer's home studio, the 'Upstairs at Harry's' of the CD credits, the main sessions, which incorporated a complete re-writing of the second half of the album, happened in a recording space Latimer built in the annexe to his house in Mountain View – 'Downstairs at Harry's'. Scherpenzeel's contributions were recorded in his home studio in Hilversum in the Netherlands, and tapes were carried back and forth across the Atlantic – amazingly, with none getting lost along the way. 'Go West' was recorded at Abbey Road during a – literal – flying visit to London, with Haydn Bendall as engineer. Both Burgess and Bass were on-site with Latimer in California, which removed at least one layer of complication. Also on site was drummer Don Harriss. The final cuts were then sent to LA for mastering by virtuoso engineer Doug Sax, the tape wizard behind three of The Doors' albums, including their 1967 debut and six of Pink Floyd's, including *The Wall*.

After its six-year gestation, *Dust And Dreams* was finally released in April 1991 and Latimer and Hoover waited anxiously to see if the gamble had paid off. 'At first, I was terrified,' recalls Latimer on *CV*, 'We hadn't been around for years, so who was going to buy it?'. They needn't have worried. Not only did the fans buy the album in healthy numbers, but the reviews were also positive and a company in Holland bought 'huge quantities' for European distribution.

To support the album, the Latimer, Bass, Burgess and Simmonds line-up went on tour in summer 1992, starting with a one-off in San Rafael, California and then travelling to Japan, continental Europe and the UK. On *CV*, Bass said of the tour:

> It was, to be honest, a real surprise for us as we really didn't know if anyone would come. After seven years, you don't know if anybody's still out there – so it was great that a lot of the gigs were sold out. I can remember standing on the stage in Amsterdam, the Paradiso; it was packed out just like the old days and people were singing along – we'd never had that before. I started to sing 'Drafted', then stopped and let the audience carry on – they knew the words.

The 'Retirement Sucks' tour is captured for posterity on the *Never Let Go* live CD. *Dust And Dreams* is, of course, a concept album, closely based on Nobel Prize-winner John Steinbeck's *Grapes of Wrath* (or, as it was mistranslated into Japanese upon publishing, 'The Angry Raisins'). The Wall Street Crash of 1929 precipitated the deepest depression in US – indeed, world – history. In 1933, at its worst level, US unemployment stood at almost 25% of the working-age population; even with the catastrophe of the Dust Bowl and lost production, crop prices fell by 60%; and there were in the region of two million homeless migrating around the nation, the majority westwards.

Against this background, California was seen as the 'land of milk and honey' – a place where work was abundant and fresh starts – and fortunes – could be made. *The Grapes of Wrath* follows a family of poor tenant farmers on their journey from Oklahoma to the promised land in the West.

Latimer, through the music, and Hoover's lyrics, capture the ups and downs, hope and despair, wide landscapes and deserted habitations of this pivotal period of American history in quite magnificent style.

Coming immediately after *Single Factor* and *Stationary Traveller*, it's a revelation – a pretty much 180 degree turn back in the direction of what makes Camel so special. As stated above, instrumentally and compositionally, *Dust And Dreams* is a *tour-de-force*. Going back to the *Snow Goose* days, Latimer uses themes and leitmotifs in such an inspirational manner.

I know I'm in danger of over-using the word, but 'masterpiece' is exactly what *Dust And Dreams* is, period. After the mostly sub-par offerings of *Stationary Traveller*, the status of *Dust And Dreams* is even further enhanced. However, in the interest of telling it how I see it, I'm going to unapologetically end the musical critique of *Dust And Dreams* with the 'elephant in the room': this conceptually, instrumentally and compositionally exceptional album is let down by the vocals. When called upon as vocalist, Latimer sings flat on too many occasions and at risk of an online flame war, I'll commit to paper a suggestion that this is one instance where the dreaded autotune might come in handy for a remaster. There: I've said it.

In reviewing the LP, I'm using a similar approach to that of *Snow Goose*, as I feel that going into some detail on the narrative pays dividends in getting more out of the music which, like *Snow Goose*, comprises extended compositions as well as short interludes. In and of themselves, these would not merit the 'full' track treatment and as is the spirit of this book, I'll try not to stray into the deep woods of musical theory – I'll focus more on things like harmonicas than harmonics.

Last but not least, if you're new to *Dust And Dreams* the piece demands to be listened to in its entirety – at least the first time around – such is its coherence and completeness.

'Dust Bowl' (Latimer)
Barn doors banging in the wind, window shutters clattering, maybe a tumbleweed skittering across the prairie, dust devils spiralling. Cattle skulls litter the fields of failed crops.

With a suitably solemn and atmospheric synth and piano intro, we commence our musical journey into the past. Ominously, a vulture calls overhead.

'Go West' (Latimer)
Although the lyrics are credited to Latimer with 'Go West', I suspect that Hoover also had a hand in their development. As an American, she closely

identified with the history of the depression-era USA and no doubt had read *Grapes of Wrath* at school, so would have been able to add an important stamp of authenticity to the words. Hoover or not, 'Go West' is accomplished poetry: 'It was the very edge of summer, the air was thin, the sky more pale. Dusty roads, I remember. Oh so well' – it's lovely stuff, and both Latimer and Hoover's lyrics – she is credited on two tracks – continue to paint a vivid picture throughout the record.

Minor key piano chords back Latimer's mournful vocals recounting the story of the protagonists being evicted along with the landowners – the farm being repossessed, a muted accompaniment absolutely in keeping with the subject matter. It's only seconds from the end of the song that we hear Latimer's guitar, and already there are rays of hope on the horizon.

'Dusted Out' (Latimer)

With a very Tony Banks-like grand piano backed by lush strings, timpani, brass and a choir, the 'Dusted Out' interlude neatly ends the first section. The title is a clever double-meaning, referring to the inescapable fug of the dust bowl itself as well as to the family being 'dusted out' of their home in front of a large metaphorical broom.

'Mother Road' (Latimer)

'Dust Bowl', 'Go West' and 'Dusted Out' are, in effect, the overture to *Dust And Dreams*. With 'Mother Road' – a direct reference to US Route 66, the legendary road the Joad family take on their drive from Oklahoma to California – now we're off west in earnest, and Latimer's howling guitar licks give more than just a nod to the likes of Molly Hatchet and southern rock in general – complete with a thumping 4/4 backbeat.

Then (at 2:18), after a couple of teasing instrumental bars and a modulation into the major key comes the first iteration of the main *Dust And Dreams* theme, and what a riff it is: tremendous, uplifting, a classic. Following soon after this is Latimer at his bluesy best, knocking out licks and power chords with abandon – astonishing stuff, and then there's suddenly a change of mood as we hear portentous chords on a fairground organ. Multi-sectioned, varied tempos, key changes. This is Camel alright, back on the straight and narrow – and we're just at the start of an incredible four-album run.

'Mother Road' has carved out a regular spot in the live sets and the band visibly love rocking out to the blues: with Pete Jones now in the line-up, the addition of his Hammond to the song in an extended jam is staggeringly good.

'Needles' (Latimer)

On reaching California, the Joad family are swiftly moved on by the police, saying that the locals 'Don't like 'Okies''. Ahead of them is a vast expanse of desert, and the last gas station is in Needles, a one-horse town on the border with Arizona.

The foreboding tone at the end of 'Mother Road' continues, indicating the vista the family are looking at: hundreds of miles of empty desert and a pick-up truck on its last legs to get them across it. We hear the harmonica, briefly, for the first time, adding to the evocation of a hopeless situation and then more of the choir, with the second *Dust And Dreams* theme hinted at on piano.

'Rose Of Sharon' (Latimer, Hoover)
There's a baby a comin': this track features a gorgeous operatic duet between David Paton as Connie Rivers and Mae McKenna as his wife, the titular Rose of Sharon. The whole arrangement, from the voices to the strings to the piano in the background, is staggering in its beauty. Then comes Latimer, channelling Mark Knopfler with his stunning tone during the bridge, and right on cue, the duet returns for one more verse. The 'Go West' theme briefly returns before the outro comprising piano and crickets.

Scottish vocalist Mae McKenna, the mother of Jamie Woon, who had a minor but critically acclaimed UK hit with 'Night Air' in 2010, was a jobbing singer that did the rounds in the Celtic folk-rock world. She was also to appear in the more genre-appropriate *Harbour Of Tears*, but without Paton as a foil, which is a pity: they work together so very well.

'Milk 'n' Honey' (Latimer)
The previous number's outro becomes the intro for 'Milk 'n' Honey'. Them pesky crickets are still around and there's a solo keyboard variation on the 'what you gonna do' theme. This ambient instrumental interlude encapsulates the hopelessness of traversing the Mojave Desert in search of that 'land of milk and honey', then suddenly on harmonica, we get a minor-key variation on the main theme – a perfect segue that introduces some delightful orchestration, with a subtle call back to 'Go West'. The family have reached their planned destination. End of act one.

'End Of The Line' (Latimer, Hoover)
With the first actual pause between tracks, the Second Act narrative commences. The family moves from camp to camp, standing in line both in the hope of finding work and being fed from the soup kitchens.

'End Of The Line' is a slow burner right out of the top drawer, the drama heightened by Latimer's plaintive vocals. Once the tempo builds, there are clever little interjections from the Hammond and Latimer lets loose starting with a tremendous solo between the second and third verses, and the soloing continues throughout the rest of the song, interspersed with the vocals.

'Storm Clouds' (Latimer)
From here on in – essentially the last third of the album – it's instrumentals all the way, so we're back deep into *Snow Goose* territory and inevitably, there are parallels to be drawn with the 1975 classic. I remain puzzled regarding

why Hoover and Latimer chose to end the lyrical content so soon as the story has much more to come, providing loads of opportunity to pen additional words.

However, it is what it is, and Latimer's compositional and arranging genius do the job admirably. He is, after all, more comfortable as an instrumentalist than a vocalist. 'Storm Clouds' does a great job conjuring up the vision of an approaching thunderstorm with deep organ notes representing the thunder, twinkling synths mimic the rain starting to fall and slide guitar squeals become the lightning. The storm is a pivotal moment in the story, as it indicates the end of the California growing season and the prospect of unemployment until the following spring.

'Cotton Camp' (Latimer)
The cotton camp of the title was the last stop on the family's journey, and by now, Grandma and Grandpa are dead. After a murderous fight at the camp, Tom is on the lam; soon after, Connie disappears, abandoning Rose of Sharon to the final weeks of her pregnancy: she still believes he will return, the others not so much.

Starting where 'Storm Clouds' left off with a couple of bars of ambient and atmospheric synths, 'Cotton Camp' soon introduces another theme, this time an uplifting melody: there's hope – and income – on the horizon. There's also – love 'em or hate 'em – 'gated' drums. Needless to say, Latimer soars above the intricate keyboard parts and the mixing is excellent considering that Scherpenzeel played his parts remotely from the main sessions, with the tapes crisscrossing both the continental USA and the Atlantic – a round trip of almost 18,000km.

'Broken Banks' / 'Sheet Rain' / 'Whispers' (Latimer)
The family have found a home in a boxcar near a creek, but as a result of the heavy winter rains, the banks have burst and the water is rising close to their shelter. This is the most orchestral passage of the LP, insistent pizzicato strings doing a fine job as raindrops while thunder rumbles in the background. At the close of the 'Sheet Rain' section, there's a beautiful string and woodwind arrangement (here the technology shines as the synthesized orchestrations are pretty much indistinguishable from the real thing) that ends with a couple of references to the main theme on harmonica. Then the oboe comes in to represent Rose of Sharon whispering to her newborn, first unaware of what has happened...

'Little Rivers And Little Rose' (Latimer)
...the baby is stillborn. 'Little Rivers and Little Rose' is a showcase for Bass on fretless layered over an insistent keyboard figure – the tension is palpable as Rose of Sharon, in denial, starts to come to terms with the tragedy. Once more, we hear the plaintive harmonica ...

'Hopeless Anger' (Latimer)

... and then a sudden change of dynamics and pace. Musically, things just get better and better all the way to the end. The family has had to move to higher ground and seek shelter in an old barn. There, they find a boy and his father, who is dying of starvation. In a scene of excruciating pathos, as the only way to save the man, Rose of Sharon feeds him with her breast milk. 'Hopeless Anger' is an incredible, multi passage composition that returns to the main theme – a real barnstormer – appropriate, I suppose since we've had a barn and a storm. Latimer and the band really go for it on this, which is, in my opinion, the most complete song since 'Echoes'. Ending with a mighty wallop on the kettle drum, this is a live favourite and justly so.

'Whispers In The Rain' (Latimer)

Latimer's questioning guitar overlays multiple references to themes and motifs from earlier in the piece, underpinned by more of that gorgeous orchestration. And so it ends, the story – like the music – unresolved. I'll say it again just for the record: *Dust And Dreams* is a masterpiece.

Harbour Of Tears (1996)

Personnel:
Andrew Latimer: guitar, vocals, keyboards, pennywhistle
Colin Bass: bass, backing vocals
Mickey Simmonds: keyboards
Additional musicians
John Xepoleas: drums, percussion
David Paton: bass, lead vocals on 'Send Home the Slates'
Mae McKenna: a capella vocal on 'Irish Air'
Neil Panton: oboe, soprano sax, harmonium
Barry Phillips: cello
John Burton: French horn
James SK Wăn: bamboo flute (not credited on the sleeve)
Karen Bentley: violin
Anita Stoneham: violin
Produced by Andy Latimer at Downstairs at Harry's
Engineers: Andy Latimer, Colin Bass (mixing), Chris Now (editing and mastering)
Release date: 15 January 1996
Running time: 62:14
Current edition: Camel Productions CP-006CD
Highest Chart Places: did not chart

Harbour of Tears is the second of the Mountain View albums before Latimer and Hoover moved to the Pacific coast and the second concept album on the bounce (third, if you must count *Stationary Traveller*). Latimer developed the concept as a result of the death of his father. He tells the story on *CV*:

> In 1993 my father died, and as you can imagine, it was quite a profound experience. I was there at his bedside, and I started to think about his side of the family and I realised that I didn't really know much about it. I discovered that my mother was Irish and I found out that she came from this place called Queenstown, which was also known as Cobh [pronounced 'cove'] Harbour. Cobh Harbour was locally known as 'The Harbour of Tears' because it was the last sight of their homeland that the Irish saw before they emigrated to the USA and Canada: the title struck me immediately.

In fact, Cobh was the departure point for 2.5 million of the six million Irish people who emigrated to North America between 1848 – three years after the start of the catastrophic Potato Famine – and 1950, as well as being the final port of call for the RMS Titanic before she set out on her fateful journey across the Atlantic.

After carrying out some more far-reaching family history research, Latimer discovered that his maternal grandmother was one of those that had left for

America from Cobh, never to return. A blood connection thus made, he states on *CV* that he immediately decided to dedicate the album to his recently-deceased father:

> I wrote a little theme for my dad and when I listened to the whole album, I thought, 'my dad's all over this' – it comes in and out across the whole album: it wasn't a conscious effort at all. So, it's a very personal album.

The story is seen from the perspective of three main characters: a father figure, who stays in Ireland, one of his seven sons who travels to the USA to work on the transcontinental railroad, and his childhood sweetheart, who remains in Ireland as a linen weaver, but longs to join him.

Although not quite the cast of thousands recruited for *The Single Factor*, nevertheless, it's quite a roster of musicians. In addition to Latimer, Bass, Paton and Simmonds, renowned Californian educator and session drummer John Xepoleas joins on drums and percussion and Mae McKenna, Rose of Sharon from *Dust And Dreams*, returns in a more genre-appropriate role. Completing the line up is a small classical ensemble including, on cello, Barry Phillips, who would return for a key role on *Rajaz*.

Latimer, Bass, Foss Patterson and Dave Stewart toured the album and this is captured on the *Coming of Age* live CD. Given *Harbour Of Tears'* complicated arrangements and orchestration, the fact that they pulled it off in style with just four of them on stage is nothing short of incredible. As for *Dust And Dreams*, this one needs to be listened to the whole way through, at least the first time around.

'Irish Air' / 'Irish Air' (Instrumental Reprise) (traditional Gaelic / Latimer)

Mae McKenna sings a 19th Century Irish Air, a capella in the purest of Celtic-inflected voices: there's no question where we are – The Emerald Isle. Latimer enters, firstly on acoustic guitar cleverly processed to sound like a Celtic harp, overlaid by flute playing the Irish Air melody. A short solo, again following the melody, and backed by lush strings, transitions into a compact marching band section with the Penny Whistle, this time taking the melody. A solo variation on the theme closes the overture; the scene is perfectly set.

'Harbour Of Tears' (Latimer)

Latimer's voice is back on track; in fact, it never sounded better. The plodding beat suggests drudgery and despair, and the lyrical content is suitably melancholy as a father says farewell to his sons from the quayside. The second verse brings with it some wonderful harmony singing from Latimer, Bass and Paton. The measured beat continues throughout, the song closing with an old-school Latimer guitar solo, heavy on the sustain. We hear a few seagulls in the background.

'Cóbh' (Interlude) (Latimer, Hoover) / 'Send Home The Slates' (Latimer, Hoover)

Pronounced 'cove', this port was until 1920 known as Queenstown, but you know Anglo-Irish politics and all that. Thus far, it's been minor key all the way, but after a few bars of this cinematic interlude, the music modulates into the major and we segue into 'Send Home The Slates'. The 'slates' refer to Irish slang meaning the son will send home money to pay the rent and clear the family's debts in Ireland. David Paton takes the lead vocal, his Scottish accent somewhat at odds with the subject matter, but nonetheless, he makes a good stab at sounding like one of his Celtic neighbours from across the sea. Bass takes the role of railroad foreman in the middle section, chivvying the navvies along and promising 'double pay' should they get the stretch of line finished on schedule.

After some classic Latimer soloing, Paton is back for the final verse and a 'p.s.' to his ma, enclosing a photo and entreating the family to not forget him.

'Under The Moon' (Interlude) (Latimer) / 'Watching The Bobbins' (Latimer, Hoover)

Latimer plays another variation on the 'Irish Air' theme, backed by subtle orchestrations, setting us up for the first classic on the album, 'Watching The Bobbins'. Very Floyd-y to start with, with hints of Porcupine Tree's 'Voyage 34' and Genesis' 'Driving The Last Spike', 'Bobbins' introduces a second protagonist, the girlfriend of our hero who is 'saving every penny she earns' in order to make the fare to America and join her beau. A new theme is introduced with chorused guitar, the unshifting rhythm encapsulating the movement of shuttles, treadles and other machinery, as well as the monotony of working 'ten hours a day' in an Irish linen weaving factory.

After the vocal content, for the second half of the song, it's blues to the fore Latimer-style, interspersed with a few parps from the Hammond, leading into tremendous synth and rhythm section interplay and guitar soloing over the top. It is copybook multi-section Camel magnificence.

'Generations' (Interlude) (Latimer) / 'Eyes Of Ireland' (Latimer, Hoover)

Heavily orchestrated, with no soloing, with this interlude the music is back in a minor key. Many years have passed, and still living in the USA, our protagonist regales, presumably, his sons with tales of the old country and his departure from the Harbour of Tears where he had his 'last eyes of Ireland'. Acoustic guitar prevails throughout, and Hoover's storytelling is delightful with references to the good times, then the potato famine, as well as namechecking the 'little people' (Fae) along the way. A compact penny whistle figure closes the number.

'Running From Paradise' (Latimer)

Commencing with epic timpani rolls and lavish strings that imply a momentous decision is to be made, this is the second 'keeper' on *Harbour Of Tears*. There are no lyrics this time; the music is left to do the storytelling. Given the title and then the lyrics of the next track 'End Of The Day', my interpretation of this is that our hero is going to return to his homeland. Latimer plays some portentous slide guitar before Simmonds comes in on piano and we start to hear the Irish Jig, slide guitar and penny whistle intertwined, in all its glory. This jig comprises the mid-section of 'Running From Paradise' and the studio version is quite restrained – cinematic, even – but the live version on *Coming Of Age* is a killer – the band really let loose, and you get a real party-in-a-barn feeling with Foss Patterson outstanding on keys.

The third, admittedly lovely piano-led section, to me, seems out of place tacked on to this song. I'm not sure what it's trying to say or portray: maybe it's the prospect of a journey back to Ireland coloured by mixed emotions?

'End Of The Day' (Latimer, Hoover)
Hoover's compact lyric is gorgeous. As I intimated above, this does to me suggest that the son has returned home and the Irishness of the main theme underscores the image.

'Coming Of Age' (Latimer)
'Alright: I'm now a grown-up. After my salad days in the USA, I now need to own my life' is what 'Coming Of Age' suggests to me. The music shouts 'determination' from start to finish and although there's one more song to come on the album, this is properly the grand finale to *Harbour of Tears*. I love the uplifting middle section, but you have to admit that it's more than a touch Genesis-y for a few minutes. Latimer's glissando work that comes in at the 4:40 mark is earth-shatteringly brilliant – it's a passage of extreme complexity that he pulls off without a sweat and is able to deliver live in spades as well.

'The Hour Candle (A Song For My Father)' (Latimer)
Again we clearly hear the 'da dah da, da dah da' motif that Latimer wrote for his father, a theme that pops up throughout the piece. A guitar solo of heart-string-tugging poignancy forms the centrepiece of 'The Hour Candle', and it's right up there with 'Ice' and 'Sahara' as one of Latimer's finest moments. He has never become the 'guitar hero' that John Tobler from the *NME* predicted back in 1976, but like us, those who know, know.

Irish pipes and massed snare drums bring the story almost to a close, then McKenna reprises the 'Irish Air' to a backdrop of waves and seagulls: don't be misled by the 23:01 duration that your device is telling you, the meat and potatoes of this wonderful track are over at the eight-minute mark and the tale of the following fifteen minutes is as follows. Latimer, on *CV*:

I put some waves at the end of the album – and the guy I was working with said 'you can put on another twenty minutes of waves if you like – you've got the space' and I thought what a fantastic idea, it'll give people time to relax and reflect on what they've heard, to absorb the harbour sounds – but of course there's always people who say 'why didn't you put more music on the LP, what's all these waves about?' So it's a mixed thing about having [the space on a CD for] a long album.

Indeed it is, Andy, indeed it is.

Camel were great at keeping fans up to date through the medium of their *Nature of the Beast* newsletter, this one from 1999. (*Private collection of Shane Carlson*)

Rajaz (1999)

Personnel:
Andrew Latimer: guitar, vocals, flute, keyboards, percussion
Colin Bass: bass
Ton Scherpenzeel: keyboards
Dave Stewart: drums, percussion
Barry Phillips: cello
Produced by Andy Latimer at Little Barn Studios, Pescadero, CA, USA
Engineers: Andy Latimer, Joe Sigretto, Ken Lee
Release date: 21 October 1999
Running time: 58:06
Current edition: Camel Productions CP009CD
Highest chart places: did not chart

By now, Latimer and Hoover had moved some 40 miles from Mountain View. They found an amazing plot of land overlooking the Pacific coast in Pescadero, built their dream house and then created a custom recording studio in the barn on the property – Little Barn Studios. Life is full of coincidences, and as Andy Latimer confirmed to me in March 2021, he and Susan Hoover were unaware that the town was the childhood home of Gordon Moore, co-founder and chairman emeritus of Intel and the author of the cardinal 'Moore's Law' about computer chip power. His childhood home, which still stands in the town, is called 'Lunasea'. Andy and Susan were fated to live in Pescadero.

501 Bean Hollow Road – it's right there on Google Earth, and you can see a photo in the colour section – also had enough land for Hoover to indulge her passion for horse-riding, a hobby that very nearly cost her life. On 6 August 2000, she was out riding when her horse got spooked and threw her. She sustained critical injuries, including two broken hips, but providentially ex-Jethro Tull drummer Clive Bunker, hired after Dave Stewart's departure, was at the house rehearsing for the *Rajaz* tour and saw what had happened. As Bunker's wife owned stables back in the UK, he was familiar and comfortable around horses and managed to calm it down and call for help. Susan was airlifted to hospital for emergency surgery and thankfully fully recovered.

To compound the situation, as mentioned above, the band were rehearsing for the *Rajaz* tour and as manager, Hoover was for the moment unable to carry on with the planning, plus it had become apparent that Bunker wouldn't be touring after all as he wasn't able to reliably hold the beat for some of the more complicated songs in odd time signatures. Talking with me in 2021, Colin Bass recounted what happened next:

When I arrived at San Francisco Airport, Andy was waiting and so was Clive, which I thought was nice. Then Clive said 'I'm going home' – which, as you can imagine, was a bit of a shock as I'd recommended him in the first place: he'd been there alone with Andy, but it hadn't gone well.

115

Therefore the hunt was on to find a drummer for the tour just two weeks before the warm-up gig in Tahoe City: marvellous. Luckily Guy LeBlanc, who had been recruited for the tour due to Ton Scherpenzeel's inability to fly, knew someone who was available and might fit the bill, so he called fellow Canadian Denis Clement. Denis was an unknown quantity to all except Guy, but nevertheless, he flew down, sat behind the kit in rehearsals and the rest, as they say, is history.

To learn more about the trials and tribulations that continued to plague the *Rajaz* tour, it's all laid out in excruciating detail in the sleeve notes to *The Paris Collection* live CD: best you sit down with a stiff drink before digesting the contents.

Meanwhile, drama out of the way, let's get back to the music. With twelve LPs under their belts, this was the first time the band wrote an album that actually had something to do with camels. Rajaz is an ancient Arabic form of poetry, and although similar in pronunciation, is not in any way related to the Pakistani 'ragas' popularised by Nusrat Fateh Ali Khan. Rajaz is characterised by a rhythm that is supposed to resemble the gait of a camel and is used to great effect in many of the tracks on the album.

An additional inspiration for this foray into world music was Bass's concurrent involvement with the 3 Mustaphas 3, already covered in the 'Cast Of Characters' section.

The Little Barn was equipped with the latest and greatest technology, including a 24-Track desk and two-inch tape machine. As for the next album, *A Nod And A Wink*, the resultant sound is extremely expansive, rich and full with the technology also enabling the master to be encoded in HDCD. Replicating the process of the first two California albums, drummer and bassist flew in for the sessions, and as with *Dust And Dreams*, Scherpenzeel's contributions were recorded in his studio in Holland and couriered to Latimer.

All of the *Rajaz* songs are longer-form compositions, with nothing under five minutes and 'Lawrence' clocking in at over ten, contrasting with the previous two that had multiple sub-five minute compositions and short 'interludes': *Rajaz*, I think, really benefits from this approach, even though broadly speaking it is a sort of concept album but without a consistent narrative.

Ultimately, *Rajaz* is all about rhythm and soundscapes, and it achieves that goal to perfection.

'Three Wishes' (Latimer)

A whoosh of wind and a mesmeric, syncopated, pulsating beat that evokes heat haze shimmering off endless sand dunes; a tinkle of wind chimes heralds the appearance of a genie and his titular offering. With an opening guitar figure reminiscent of 'Shine On You Crazy Diamond', the tension slowly rises as the drums come in and then – what a peach of a main riff, Latimer doing what he does best – such a clean, melodic and expressive sound. I defy you not to have a smile put on your face listening to this melody.

The middle section, with its chorused glissando guitar interplaying with Scherpenzeel's restrained synth arpeggios, is a peach that leads into a short third section employing chord changes like the old days as well as some subtle North African figures and handclapping, followed by a couple of bars of organ brazenly nicked from early Genesis. But so what – it's great. Remember that Ton wasn't in the studio with the rest of the guys, so the editing and mixing is remarkable.

One of only two instrumentals on *Rajaz*, 'Three Wishes' is multi-section and neo-symphonic in scale – this is the most Camelly Camel has been since 1976. Anyone who gave up after *Moonmadness* should now be happy to reacquaint themselves with the band – stirring stuff. As a Camel fan, 'Three Wishes' should be familiar like your favourite fluffy blanket: just wrap yourself up in it and feel the warmth; as an album opener, it promises much, and fear not, the band delivers on that promise.

'Lost And Found' (Latimer, Hoover)
Latimer's unprocessed and exceptionally clear voice, for once front and centre in the mix, works well. With its lolloping beat, the first song on the album to hint at the Rajaz of the title, 'Lost and Found', features great arranging throughout with Californian Barry Phillips on cello. At the time, he was a student of world-famous sitar virtuoso Ravi Shankar, making him the perfect bowsman to participate in the Eastern influence of the music.

Three-odd minutes of mid-section is vintage stuff comprising solos from both Latimer and Scherpenzeel (channelling Wakeman) and Bass harmonising smartly on bass. A short bridge heralds a reprise of the original theme, this time without vocals, but instead a heavily-sustained guitar line.

It's difficult to fathom what Hoover's enigmatic lyrics are referring to. Is this an affirmation that the magic of early Camel has been rediscovered as Latimer's creativity found a new lease of life, or is it simply a forlorn-yet-hopeful affirmation of seizing the day as one gets older? I'll leave it up to you to find your own meaning.

'The Final Encore' (Latimer)
Rhythm is vital to everything on *Rajaz*, and never more so than for 'The Final Encore'. It plods along – in a good way, mind – in a meter brilliantly replicating a camel's progress through the sand: plod, plod, plod …

Latimer's slide guitar – a technique for which he rarely seldom gets the plaudits he deserves – features front and centre here during an extended introduction. When the vocals come in, again, Andy's voice is right up front and sounds great. A guitar solo that starts in very Middle Eastern fashion melds into a typical Latimer melodic figure – a cute touch that brings two worlds together.

The orchestration throughout is mellifluous and perfectly-judged. With no classicists on hand during the sessions – apart from the cellist – this is all down to Scherpenzeel's encyclopaedic knowledge of what was possible with synths, as is the all-too-brief 'mizmar' (Arabic oboe) motif at the 6:40 mark.

Once again, Hoover's cryptic lyrics raise more questions than answers. This most certainly wasn't Camel's 'final encore', so maybe mysticism is all it's meant to be, given the theme.

'Rajaz' (Latimer, Hoover)

A strumming acoustic guitar and vocals are all we hear, giving no indication of the scale of what is to come. Phillips' cello joins the guitar for the second verse, and still no hint of what's to follow. At this stage, it can be safely assumed that this will be an acoustic number, and that's not dispelled as Latimer takes up the flute for a short pastoral interlude. But wait: what's this? An electric guitar and that same, steady, lolloping beat we were introduced to in 'Final Encore'? Camel have done it again – a magnificently constructed, multi-section masterpiece.

During the track's eight minutes, fully half is a showcase for Latimer's inimitable guitar which seamlessly veers from delta blues slide work to full-on Chicago blues wail to melodic rock: the man's a genius.

The lyrics are, of course, structured in Rajaz form, following the beat exactly, telling us about a night-time caravan of camels crossing the desert, with the stars overhead as 'the souls of heaven' – lovely poetry from the pen of Hoover.

Played live in recent years, the song features Peter Jones playing a show-stopping extended sax solo that raises 'Rajaz' to a new level of epic-ness and is a perfect example of how his joining the band has brought additional dimensions to the back catalogue.

'Shout' (Latimer, Hoover)

Shout, the most compact track on the album, is a mid-tempo stomp complete with rim shots, strumming and minimal soloing that sounds rather ... OK, *very* 1980s Dire Straits in places, so the number feels just a little bit out of place on *Rajaz*. Latimer's plaintive vocals do justice to the subject matter, an apology of sorts from a musician to an unspecified friend, but I refuse to believe it's about either Bardens or Ward, no matter how some of the words might resonate with each of those characters. No, the lyrics of 'Shout' remain an enigma, so let's leave it that way.

'Straight To My Heart' (Latimer)

Clearly autobiographical – the lyrics are Latimer's alone and he was indeed born in '49 – 'Straight To My Heart' is another showcase for his tremendous guitar skills, supported ably and sympathetically by the band. The 'red guitar' is, of course, the Fender Stratocaster that he plays to this day and the call back to Radio Luxembourg – the original European 'pirate' radio station that was the catalyst to a lifelong love of rock for many whose formative years were in the 60s and 70s – is an evocative touch for us of a 'certain age'.

Like 'Shout', there's no obvious tie-back to the *Rajaz* concept, but that's put right on 'Sahara', the next track on our journey across the desert.

'Sahara' (Latimer)

No ifs or buts, the penultimate track 'Sahara' is staggeringly good old school Camel. Like opener 'Three Wishes', no other band sounds like this or has even tried. Right from the jazz-inflected, Metheny-like opening section, Latimer's guitar tone never sounded better and then off he goes on his golden Les Paul into the six-string stratosphere. The pacing of 'Sahara' is spot-on, with tempo changes aplenty. During Latimer's almost three-minute solo, we hear more of those Arabic figures, which imperceptibly shift into a more western rock vibe, ending with precise glissando and choral chanting, courtesy of Scherpenzeel's synth Mellotron sample. Is the solo as good as that on 'Ice'? Yes, I think it is.

'Lawrence' (Latimer, Hoover)

Unsurprisingly, the most cinematic song on *Rajaz* is 'Lawrence', a reference to the larger-than-life 'Lawrence of Arabia', the subject of multiple biographies and the epic David Lean movie. Hoover, however, takes liberties with the lyrics as in actuality, T. E. Lawrence died as a result of a motorcycle accident back in the UK, and not by being 'swallowed by the sand'. In fact, the lyrics are more suited to the legend of Paul Atreides of the *Dune* novels (*Dune Messiah*, to be precise), but I digress.

Unquestionably symphonic in execution, what with its lush strings and choir of the opening, as well as being the longest track on *Rajaz*, 'Lawrence', lyrical liberties notwithstanding, is a worthy tribute to an undoubtedly great historical character. Lengthy though the track is, in line with all of Camel's ten-minute-plus compositions, it doesn't come over as being over-wrought or padded with filler material and naturally, Latimer's guitar is sublime throughout.

As for so many of Camel's album closers – 'Ice', 'Lady Fantasy' and 'Lunar Sea' immediately spring to mind – it leaves the listener craving for more. Three years later, we'd get just that, in the form of *A Nod And A Wink*.

A Nod and a Wink (2002)

Personnel:
Andrew Latimer: guitar, flute, vocals
Guy LeBlanc: keyboards, backing vocals
Colin Bass: bass, vocals
Denis Clement: drums, percussion
Additional musicians
Terry Carleton: drums ('Simple Pleasures', 'Squigely Fair'), percussion, backing vocals ('For Today')
JR Johnston: Backing vocals ('For Today')
Produced by Andy Latimer at Little Barn Studios, Pescadero, CA, USA
Engineers: Andy Latimer, Joe Sigretto, Ken Lee
Release date: 19 July 2002
Running time: 55:34
Current edition: Camel Productions (CP-013CD)
Highest Chart Places: Did not chart

Twenty-six years later, and at last, Camel delivered an album to rival the first four. Lined up with the previous three recordings, lovely though they are, this is the one that sounds the most 'Camelly' since *Moonmadness*. The Second of the Little Barn LPs, *A Nod And A Wink* was recorded from April to June 2002.

The album is also the most English-sounding in character since *Breathless*, so by this time, maybe Latimer and Hoover were starting to feel a little homesick for England's green and pleasant land. Overall it's a reflective record and full of wonderful moments, with Latimer's flute a real feature on many cuts.

After touring *Rajaz*, Guy LeBlanc and Denis Clement were now fixtures in the band, joining Latimer and Bass as a compact four-piece, the first time Camel had this shape – believe it or not – since *Moonmadness*. Bay Area freelance drummer Terry Carleton took percussion duty, including the glockenspiel heard on the title track, and filled in for Clement at The Little Barn when the Canadian was unavailable due to other commitments, also providing backing vocals on 'For Today'. As for *Rajaz*, the CD is encoded for HDCD, bringing out the full dynamics of the compositions.

Given Peter Bardens' untimely death in the January of 2002, Latimer dedicated the album to him: I think Pete would see it as a fitting memorial. At the time of writing, this is the most recent studio album from Camel. Will it be the last? Only time, and Latimer's desire to enlarge his musical legacy, will tell.

'A Nod And A Wink' (Latimer, Hoover, LeBlanc)

Chuff, chuff, chuff – off goes the steam train from a rural station that's straight out of an Agatha Christie whodunnit?. As the train disappears into the rolling English countryside, a be-smocked and dishevelled yokel plays his penny whistle, a wheat stem hangs from the corner of his mouth, a flagon of cider is no doubt nearby. The atmosphere is no less than feeling we're being transported to the British children's TV show *Camberwick Green*.

'A Nod And A Wink' is a lullaby with a difference, but it starts off conventionally enough with the lyrics exhorting someone, presumably a child, to 'climb the wooden hill': 'baa baa black sheep' and a bar-or-four of Dad's jolly whistling to lull us into never-never land. Then bam! Power chords, baby!

Right from the off, everything hangs together perfectly in another archetypal multi-section Camel masterwork. Latimer's chorused soloing that switches back and forth with slide without him catching his breath – he does it so bloody well – is something to behold. LeBlanc shines, particularly on Hammond, and with Clement we have a drummer with punch and drive at last filling the sneakers of Andy Ward.

'A Nod And A Wink' has plenty of dynamic shifts and catchy riffs throughout, the discords in the middle section presumably indicate REM sleep or a nightmare, but I do take issue with some of the lyrics – 'carpets of magic' is a somewhat clumsy lyric, reverse-engineered just to make the verse scan.

At the risk of stating the obvious, the 'Nod' of the title is 'nodding off' and the 'Wink' 'forty winks', but there's also an English idiom, immortalised by Eric Idle of Monty Python, 'A nod's as good as a wink to a blind bat' – so this is cunning wordplay that I fully support. Not since 'Scenes From A Night Dream' on Genesis' *And Then There Were Three...* have we been on such an enjoyable prog somnambulation. As for many Camel songs, its ten-plus minutes are over all too soon. Summing up, 'A Nod And A Wink' is, to paraphrase that sage of all things rock, Mr Nigel Tufnel, 'none more Camel'.

'Simple Pleasures' (Latimer, Hoover)

Opening with a programmed drumbeat and percussion that's a dead ringer for the opening bars of Genesis' 'Silver Rainbow' off *Mama*, the I'm-sure-unwitting plagiarism aside, it works beautifully all the same. Latimer's melancholy tones fit the subject matter like a glove and lyrically, Hoover delivers in spades. This one is real poetry, with its Proustian nuance and memories of distant loves and years.

Bluesy guitar licks punctuate the vocals, with that sequenced beat continuing until the band arrives in full-on blues-funk mode: it's a tremendously effective change of pace and style, reminiscent of *On The Beach*-era Chris Rea.

'Simple Pleasures' is a real gem that wears its five and a half minutes lightly.

'A Boy's Life' (Latimer, Hoover)

This one is the nearest Camel has ever got to folk music. Strummed acoustic guitar, at one point sounding like a mandolin, increases the effect, only for this slow build to transform into something completely different, a rolling, somewhat ambient passage. What's up? Then a new theme, based on a traditional English folk tune, emerges on acoustic and flute, pastoral in the extreme, not giving anything away about what happens next.

What *does* happen next is one of the most elegant neo-symphonic rock passages in the Camel catalogue, a lilting guitar-led rhapsody coupled with interjections from keys, lovely walking bass lines, and exceptional swinging drums. Stirring stuff.

'Fox Hill' (Latimer, Hoover)
I'm going to own up, here: 'Fox Hill' is my personal favourite Camel number since 'Lunar Sea'. Everything about this song just screams 'CAMEL' to me – the humour, the storytelling – brilliantly realised by Latimer on vocals – the multi-movement structure and, of course, the playing. I could watch the live version, with Bass on vocals (captured on the *In From the Cold* DVD, and also watchable on Camel Productions' YouTube channel) a thousand times and not ever get bored of it.

This tale (tail?) of a crafty fox sticking two furry toes up at a somewhat hapless horseman is fun from beginning to end. Hoover's lyrics – she is a keen horsewoman after all – ooze authenticity.

Back to that multi-movement structure, how does he do it time and again? Compositionally 'Fox Hill' should be in the syllabus of any self-respecting music school or degree program – I'm continually in awe of Latimer's ability in this respect. Even more so than 'White Rider', 'Echoes' and 'Lawrence' – three other individual (that is, not concept album) songs in the canon with a clear narrative – 'Fox Hill' squarely hits the mark as story in musical form. In the end, 'It's only fox and foal', but I like it.

'The Miller's Tale' (Latimer, Hoover)
Have I mentioned pastoral in respect of this album? With its birdies chirping intro, it doesn't get any more bucolic than the 'The Miller's Tale', by far the shortest of the tracks on the LP. Musically, once more, it is nicely realised with only a short, wistful lyric prefacing some lovely synthesised woodwind, strings and choir. A brass band of the sort trademarked by Big Big Train serves only to add to the Englishness of this tranquil interlude.

'Squigely Fair' (Latimer)
Cock-a-doodle-do: wake up, we're off to Squigely Fair. In case you were thinking about it, there's no point looking for the eponymous village on Google Earth as your search will be in vain – it's merely a figment of Latimer's fertile imagination. One word sums up the character of this song: jolly, as it evokes a country gathering full of jongleurs, tinkers hawking their wares (listen for the 'clink, clink, clink'), old-time mechanical carousels and all the other curiosities that might be found at a rural fair of a certain time.

Halfway through, given that the sleeve notes don't have lyrics for the song, after some subtle crowd noise, it's a surprise to hear some vocals exhorting us to 'get our tickets'. The rest of the number ambles along pleasantly, but for once, I think listeners will be content to have reached the end of the eight minutes. They've served their purpose well enough.

'For Today' (Latimer, Hoover, LeBlanc)

I really did consider just leaving this section blank as a metaphorical 'minute of silence' because the subject matter is harrowing in the extreme. 'For Today' is Hoover's reflection on the 'High Diver' of 11 September 2001 – a picture that shocked the world as it was reproduced in just about every newspaper, magazine and TV newsreel of worth. For the one and only time in this tome, I'm going to show the lyrics of a song in full:

I saw a pearl of wisdom
In the spirit of a man
As he saved
The day he lost.

Time will say I told you so
If we look back in regret.
Never give a day away.
It won't return the same again.

Nothing can last
There are no second chances.
Never give a day away.
Always live for today.

This is wonderful, gut-wrenching writing from Susan Hoover: a fitting epitaph for the unknown man.

Musically, 'For Today' treats the story with the solemnity it merits. Latimer even sounds at times like Lou Reed or Leonard Cohen in his delivery, unconsciously, I'm sure, so maybe there was a special vibe in the studio that day, as the aforementioned singers were committed New Yorkers both. Naturally, the guitar playing is perfection, with the band happy to take a supporting role, notwithstanding LeBlanc's emotional solo. Ending with multi-tracked choral voices and lavish orchestrations, we're left to reflect on that tragic day. After the shortest of pauses, the train we heard at the start of the album steams off into the distance, leaving only the sound of birds.

Associated Tracks
'After All These Years' (Latimer, LeBlanc)

This delightful instrumental, which at one point calls to mind Genesis' 'After the Ordeal' from *Selling England* ... is a bonus track on the Japanese issue. It's such a pity that this was left off the original release, available only to the Japanese, fortunate people. As the last piece of music in the Camel story thus far, it's a magnificent salutation, a potted retrospective of all that went before. Clement and Bass are in lock-step supporting Latimer's inimitably precise, melodic, expressive guitar work. LeBlanc excels on strings, Hammond and then his melancholy solo piano in the final bars is a thing of immense, intense beauty.

Postscript

Camel toured *A Nod And A Wink* during the summer and autumn of 2003: for the US part of the tour Latimer, Bass and Clement were joined by sometime Yes man Tom Brislin on keys, covering for the severely ill Guy LeBlanc on the US leg of the tour. Ton Scherpenzeel was on point for the European leg. The Corporation in Sheffield, UK, hosted the final gig of the tour on 31 October 2003. This was the last time we would see Camel on stage for almost exactly ten years. It would be Yorkshire again, but this time Harrogate, on 19 October 2013, when the magic would happen again.

In 2007, Susan Hoover delivered fans some terrible news through the medium of the Camel newsletter. By this time, the couple were back in the UK and Latimer's medical condition had become critical: he was in isolation for six weeks, but the positive energy from family, friends and fans really helped his recovery. For some considerable time afterwards, he had to take immunosuppressants to prevent his body from rejecting the bone marrow transplant that saved his life.

Speaking on *Ready to Rock* Radio in 2014, Latimer recounts how he had to relearn his vibrato technique due to arthritis, but in keeping with his incredibly positive character, he said:

> I had an image of Django Reinhardt, who was able to play with two fingers, so I knew I could do it.

On Monday 17 September 2018, almost two months to the day from the transcendental Loreley appearance, after a 43-year absence, Camel once again took to the stage at The Royal Albert Hall. A lot of water had passed under the bridge since *The Snow Goose* in 1975, the band's last appearance on that hallowed ground. One of the original members had passed away, another had come to terms with bipolar disorder, and a third had recovered from what was generally accepted at the time to be a terminal illness. But despite all of this tragedy, Camel were still relevant, selling out the venue once again to an audience of old fans as well as new ones.

It was a triumph, and if you weren't there, the music and the atmosphere of the evening are faithfully reproduced on CD, DVD and BluRay; if you were there, you experienced the magic first-hand. As we go to press, the Albert Hall performance is the last document in the Camel story, so maybe it's about time that the current rights holders reach out to a certain Mr Steven Wilson, audio engineering guru and fan as he is, with a commission to remaster the early records – at least up to *Rain Dances.* I, for one, would love to hear what he might do in particular to 'Metrognome' or 'Lunar Sea' in Dolby Atmos surround sound – it would probably blow our collective mind.

A tour was planned for 2020, but the pandemic intervened. Latimer is a renowned perfectionist, so although much new material has been written, nothing yet in his words is 'quite right'. At the time of writing, the band now regularly meet up online on Zoom, where I understand from someone very close to the band there is a great feeling of togetherness and desire to do more. Let's hope so.

When interviewed on *Progzilla* for Peter Jones' *Tales From The Tiger Moth* podcast in 2016, Andy Latimer sounded positive for the future:

> I'd like to do more in my old age, not less; people have been hoping for a new album for years. I have loads of material – I'd love to do a new album.

And then, there's the possibility of a writing collaboration between Latimer and Jones. Readers who are familiar with Pete's solo work, in the guise of Tiger Moth Tales, must see the potential here. I'm sure I speak for all of us when I say: 'Let's hope there's more to come'. It's not too late, we should never let go.

Live Albums

A Live Record (1978)

Personnel:
Andrew Latimer: guitar, vocals
Peter Bardens: keyboards, vocals
Doug Ferguson: bass, vocals
Andy Ward: drums
Mel Collins: Saxophone, flute
Richard Sinclair: bass, vocals
Produced by Rhett Davies
Release date: April 1978
Running time: 97:14 (original 1978 release), 138:06 (2002 expanded and remastered edition)
Current edition: Decca 8829282
Highest Chart Places: Did not chart

It's rare that a remastered recording gets so complete an overhaul as *A Live Record*. In fact, the changes in running order, over 40 minutes of additional content and the improvement in quality of the sound make the 2002 'Expanded and Remastered' edition a different proposition altogether, pretty much. And this is a very good thing indeed.

Regarding the running order, the revamp is intended to more closely reflect the shows on the *Rain Dances* tour, which it does, sort of. That tour, spanning the UK, Germany, Sweden and Norway, which took place in the autumn of 1977, had a *Snow Goose* section, but not the whole caboodle, as well as the inclusion of, for example, 'Tell Me' and 'Skylines', which is unsurprising given the album the tour was supporting, but apparently not sufficient to qualify for the updated live release.

As the second disc of the double album was dedicated entirely to the Royal Albert Hall recording of *Snow Goose*, the section from 'Rhayader' to 'Princess Perdue' was redundant. You can see from the setlist below, from the gig at the Glasgow Apollo on 25th September 1977, the thinking behind the new tracklisting. Also interesting to note is that 'Lady Fantasy' is not only absent as the encore but was completely missing from that tour's setlist, and that 'Never Let Go' – the opening track on the original release – was, in fact, the encore on the tour.

Sample Set List From *Rain Dances* Tour
(Glasgow Apollo 25 September 1977)

'First Light'
'Metrognome'
'Unevensong'
'Rhayader'

'Rhayader Goes To Town'
'Preparation'
'Dunkirk'
'Fritha'
'La Princess Perdue'
'Tell Me'
'Song Within A Song'
'Skylines'
'Highways Of The Sun'
'Lunar Sea'
'Rain Dances'
'One Of These Days I'll Get An Early Night'
'Never Let Go'

The finished product comprises tracks not only from the *Rain Dances* tour in 1977, but also from the Hammersmith Odeon (now the Eventim Apollo, Hammersmith) on the *Moonmadness* tour in '76 ('Chord Change') and the Marquee in October '74 ('Liggin' at Louis'' / 'Lady Fantasy') with the latter serving as the 'encore' to the non-*Snow Goose* element of the release. Also tacked on to the end of Disc two are 'The White Rider' and 'Another Night'.

'Liggin' At Louis'' (Bardens)
As the only track on *A Live Record* that can't be found anywhere else in the Camel catalogue, 'Liggin' At Louis'' merits 'the full treatment' within these pages. This Bardens number, recorded at The Marquee in London in 1974, is an odd inclusion on the album, and shows the band in full-on jazz-rock fusion mode. 'Homage to the God of Light', a bonus track on the remastered *Camel* covered earlier, comes from the same set of Marquee tapes, and listening to the two songs side by side illustrates just how close the band flirted with heading in the direction of fusion – period – before settling on the signature sound that found its feet on *Mirage*.

'Liggin' At Louis'' slopes in with a floaty synth arpeggiation, hinting that we're about to hear something a little different from the band: funky bass lines from Ferguson underline the vibe. To start with, the number is all about Bardens – switching from synths to electric piano, to Hammond and back again. Up to the three-minute mark, Latimer is all but invisible, with his strummed jazz chords *à la* renowned US guitarist and Wrecking Crew member Barney Kessel, coming forward in the mix only occasionally, but then around 3:20, he delivers with a snappy lead that echoes the main melody. After a short interlude that harks back to the opening, bang on cue at 4:40, we get a vintage Latimer solo backed by Ward's tremendous athletic drumming and cymbal work. It's fusion, folks, but inimitably Camel.

Heavy Weather, Weather Report's best-known and by far most commercially successful LP (selling more than half a million units in the first year alone), wasn't released until three years after this performance ... there's some food for thought for you.

Other Live Albums

If you're stranded on a desert island, *A Live Record* is unquestionably the one Camel live album to take with you as it showcases the original line-up as well as the early 'Caramel' period. Nevertheless, there are some gems to be unearthed in the other nine (yes, *nine*) 'official' live releases. The bootlegs freely available through the usual online outlets not only generate no income for the band, but the sound quality and presentation is uniformly rubbish. Steer well clear.

Making sense of the live releases is akin to going down Lewis Carroll's rabbit hole as many, like *A Live Record*, contain performances from more than one gig and / or year and there's a significant amount of duplication with the bonus content on the 2002 Decca and 2009 Cherry Red / Esoteric expanded remasters. Adding to the complications, the 2009 *Nude* remaster comes with the live performance of the album from the BBC airing (the broadcast itself was abridged to fit into a one-hour radio show), so it is effectively a live release in its own right.

The albums below are listed by performance date, not release date.

On the Road 1972 (Released 1992)
Venue unspecified, but possibly as support to Barclay James Harvest at The Rainbow, London, on 3 December.
Personnel:
Andrew Latimer: guitars, flute, vocals
Peter Bardens: keyboards
Doug Ferguson: bass, vocals
Andy Ward: drums
Running time: 44:18
Current edition: Camel Productions CP-003CD

A real curiosity, this. Comprising just the four tracks – 'Lady Fantasy', 'Six Ate', 'White Rider' and 'God of Light Revisited', it won't have escaped your notice that the recording is pre-the release of *Camel* in 1973, but that there are two *Mirage* numbers in the set: this being the case, why were these not laid down at Morgan and included on *Camel*? Alternatively, were they conceived in the months between the studio sessions and release date? The sound quality is as you'd expect, which is to say rather muddy.

Gods Of Light '73-'75 (Released 2000)
8 October 1973, Dingwalls Dance Hall, London, UK / BBC Radio
Personnel:
Andrew Latimer: guitars, flute, vocals
Peter Bardens: keyboards
Doug Ferguson: bass, vocals

Andy Ward: drums
Running time: 70:52
Current edition: Mooncrest CRESTCD 057 Z

This is a real antique, containing only five tracks: 'God of Light Revisited' (1973) from the *Greasy Truckers* double album, and 'White Rider', 'Lady Fantasy' and 'Arubaluba' from a BBC broadcast session 1974, and finally an excerpt from the *Snow Goose* from the 1975 BBC Radio One *In Concert* performance.

The versions of 'Arubaluba' and 'Lady Fantasy' are included on the 2009 *Mirage* remaster, but confusingly not the rendition of 'White Rider' – probably because of space, so unless you really need to hear another version of 'Gods of Light ...' or an alternative playing of the Gandalf song, then this CD is really only for completists. Sound quality is fine given the age of the original tapes, but hardly reference standard.

On The Road 1981 (Released 1997)
2 April 1981, Hammersmith Odeon, London, UK
Personnel:
Andrew Latimer: guitars, flute, vocals
Colin Bass: bass, vocals
Andy Ward: drums
Jan Schelhaas: keyboards
Kit Watkins: keyboards
Running time: 58:38
Current release: CP-007CD

A condensed setlist to fit within a one-hour *In Concert* radio broadcast from the BBC, the sound quality – as you might expect from the BBC – is excellent. 'Summer Lightning', 'Wait', 'Ice' and 'Lies' were axed, as well as the encore of 'Rhayader', 'Rhayader Goes To Town' and 'Another Night' – an understandable decision made in order to focus on the recently-released *Nude*.

However, apart from the non-*Nude* opening three tracks – 'Never Let Go', 'Song Within A Song' and 'Lunar Sea', as mentioned in the preamble, there's little reason to own this as the entire BBC *In Concert* performance of *Nude* is included on the 2009 release of *Nude*, remastered and all.

On The Road 1982 (Released 1994)
Dutch radio, 13 June 1982, Congresgebouw, The Hague, NL
Personnel:
Andrew Latimer: guitars, flute, vocals
Andy Dalby: guitar
Chris Rainbow: keyboards, vocals
Kit Watkins: keyboards
David Paton: bass, bass guitar, vocals

Stuart Tosh: drums, backing vocals
Running time: 68:41
Current edition: Camel Productions CP-005CD

This is the only surviving record of Camel's 'Tenth Anniversary Tour' (not named, you will note, the *Single Factor* tour). Infuriatingly the original tapes were lost, and so *On the Road 1982* is the sound desk capture only, in all its dubious glory: as one might expect for a desk recording, where the levels are set up for the hall and not home HiFi, the sound balance is all over the place. One plus point is that the lead vocals, from Rainbow, in particular, are clear as a bell, so hearing his take on songs from the pre-*Single Factor* catalogue is an interesting and rewarding exercise. One glaring exception to the vocal clarity is 'Wait', where something went horribly wrong.

The setlist had a smattering of *Single Factor* numbers interspersed with some choice cuts from the back catalogue, including a good rendition of 'Never Let Go' as the encore, but frankly, this is the one live album to avoid. Summing up: although in the main perfectly listenable, it's not up to the quality of the rest of the official live catalogue with the lower end especially wrapped in cotton wool wadding a couple of feet thick, so I'd argue that this one is only for completists.

Pressure Points: Live In Concert (1984 original release, 2009 expanded remaster)
11 May 1984, Hammersmith Odeon, London, UK
Personnel:
Andrew Latimer: guitars, flute, vocals
Colin Bass: bass, vocals
Paul Burgess: drums
Chris Rainbow: keyboards, vocals
Ton Scherpenzeel: keyboards
Additional musicians
Richie Close: keyboards
Mel Collins: Saxophone
Peter Bardens: Hammond organ
Running time: 84:57
Current release: Esoteric Records ECLEC22162

Pressure Points documents the *Stationary Traveller* tour and the original, single disc release was, therefore, the last output before the 'Lost Years'. The tracklisting is pretty faithful to the setlist, containing a good selection of oldies and some cherry-picked tunes from the album they were touring.

For fans, this was the gig to be at because after 'Long Goodbyes', a certain Mr Bardens sneaked on stage to perform a brace from *Snow Goose* and the encore of 'Lady Fantasy': this would be the last time he'd ever appear with the band.

Aside from the Bardens surprise and a guest appearance from Mel Collins on

'Fingertips' and 'Rhayader Goes To Town', the most interesting inclusion is set opener, 'Pressure Points', which is stretched from the two minutes of the studio version to an epic seven minutes featuring some stunning fretless work from Bass and atmospheric keyboard flourishes throughout. Although it follows the general format of the 12" single release, the mid-section is somewhat different.

The live setting somehow manages to give space to the somewhat claustrophobic nature of the *Stationary Traveller* material, which is refreshing. As stated above, the original release was a single disc affair, so be careful you buy the 2009 version to get the full enchilada.

Never Let Go (Released 1993)
5 September 1992, Enschede, Netherlands
Personnel:
Andrew Latimer: guitars, flute, vocals
Colin Bass: bass, vocals
Paul Burgess: drums
Mickey Simmonds: keyboards
Running time: 131:40
Current edition: Camel Productions CP004CD

A faithful representation of the 20th Anniversary Tour, with *Dust And Dreams* played in full, together with some classics. In fact, the first half of the gig is a chronological retrospective containing at least one track from nine of the previous ten LPs, the notable exception being *Stationary Traveller*, which was, for some reason, bypassed.

The live version of *Dust And Dreams* is tremendous, with extra dimensions added here, there and everywhere. With Bass sharing vocal duties, that side of things was taken care of too. In latter days, Camel rarely included 'Earthrise' in live sets, so this is a chance to hear an alternative rendition from the studio version on *Mirage*.

All in all, this is the one to have if you're blasé with regard to *A Live Record*.

Coming Of Age (Released 1998)
13 March 1997, Billboard, Los Angeles, USA
Personnel
Andrew Latimer: guitars, flute, vocals
Colin Bass: bass, vocals, keyboards, 12-string guitar
Dave Stewart: drums, percussion
Foss Patterson: keyboards, vocals
Running time: 124:25
Current edition: Camel Productions CP-008CD

Continuing Camel's emergent process of releasing a live album after touring the new studio release, *Coming Of Age* is the record of the *Harbour Of Tears* tour with the Latimer, Bass, Patterson and Stewart line up.

Although one of the Camel Productions 'Official Bootleg' releases, it's by no means 'bootleg' in production quality – in fact, it sounds great. As well as two mini-suites on Disc One – *Snow Goose* and *Nude* – on Disc Two, there is another mini-suite – *Dust And Dreams*, with the rest dedicated to a complete performance of *Harbour Of Tears*. There's stunning renditions of 'Lunar Sea' and 'Sasquatch' as well, which drive along at a giddy pace ably supported by the 'Fish Boys'.

The Paris Collection (Released 2001)

30 September 2000, Bataclan-Club, Paris, France.
(Note: the liner notes incorrectly state that the concert was on 30 October)
Personnel
Andrew Latimer: guitars, flute, vocals
Colin Bass: bass, vocals
Denis Clement: drums
Guy LeBlanc: keyboards
Running time: 71:03
Current edition: Camel Productions CP-011CD

This was the tour when everything went wrong but ended up being 'alright on the night', as it were: the liner notes provide all the excruciating detail you will ever need. As a stop on the *Rajaz* tour, it's strange that the CD contains only one track from that album – 'Sahara' – yet three from *Dust And Dreams*. I speculate that the only rationale for this decision was Latimer's insistence on quality, and the other *Rajaz* songs from that night didn't come up to standard: 'Three Wishes' opened the set, which also included 'Rajaz' as well as 'Echoes', 'White Rider', 'Song Within A Song', 'Watching The Bobbins', 'The Hour Candle', 'Refugee', 'Eyes Of Ireland' and 'Send Home The Slates'. As a two-CD release those could easily have been accommodated.

Tragically, the Bataclan earned its place in history on a night in November 2015 when it was attacked by terrorists. 90 music fans lost their lives.

At The Royal Albert Hall (Released 2020)

17 September 2018, Royal Albert Hall, London, UK
Personnel:
Andrew Latimer: guitars, flute, vocals
Colin Bass: Bass, vocals
Denis Clement: drums
Pete Jones: keyboards, vocals, Saxophone
Running time: 132:22
Current edition: Camel Productions CP-1015CD

The audio-only version of the sold-out landmark gig, with Latimer, Bass, Clement and Jones: read the Video section below for commentary. If you have a DVD or BluRay player, then as well as buying the CD, you should shell out on one of these too, as they come in glorious, ear-candy surround sound.

Above: Latimer in deep contemplation during 'Song Within A Song' at the Royal Albert Hall in October 2018. (*Geir Stavseng*)

Left: What a setting: view from the stage, Royal Albert Hall, October 2018. (*Geir Stavseng*)

DVDs / Blu-Rays

Camel Productions has not been backward in coming forward with video content for the faithful: there's a total of ten DVDs and one Blu-Ray to savour. The selection is a mix of archive footage, purpose-made documentary and live performances, some of them complete. Sadly, pre-*Stationary Traveller*, there are no full-concert live videos – it would have been incredible to see a complete gig with the original line-up, and then maybe something from the *Rain Dances* to *Nude* period; the *Moondances* DVD goes some way to addressing this, but it is what it is, so no point being overly wistful.

I'm deliberately not including current edition information as this is redundant: there is only one of each in the catalogue and most are available from the Camel Productions webstore.

Camel: Curriculum Vitae (DVD) (Released 2003)
A mandatory primer for all fans of the band, *Curriculum Vitae* tells the story up to and including the California reunion of Latimer, Ferguson and Ward in 2003. There's plenty of archive live footage and revealing interviews with Latimer, Bardens, Ward, Ferguson and Bass. Every phase of the band's development up to 2003 is covered in enough detail and the narrative doesn't dwell too long on any one period. Also, it's very well-paced and doesn't get lost in minutiae. Although not high-resolution, the video quality is fine as it goes: after all, it's the history we're interested in.

Pressure Points (DVD) (Released 1984)
Personnel:
Same as for the Pressure Points CD

Originally released on VHS (remember *that* format?!), the DVD begins bizarrely with photos of the band going up in flames. The live footage is interspersed with some video vignettes that are, being kind, a product of their time – but it's fun trying to figure out which band members are hamming it up: Latimer, Bass, Hoover, and Paton got dressed up for the shoot – so off you go. The video director was Mike Mansfield, helmer of promos including Grace Jones' 'Private Life', ELO's 'Mr. Blue Sky' and 'Don't Bring Me Down', and Kim Wilde's 'Love Blonde'.

Regarding the performances, as I mentioned for the CD, the live setting gives space to the *Stationary Traveller* material, and the rest of the setlist is delivered with energy and drive. However, unless you're desperate to see the acting skills of the band members, it's a far better bet to own *Total Pressure*.

Total Pressure (DVD) (Released 2006)
Personnel:
Same as for the Pressure Points CD

Total Pressure contains additional concert footage not used in the original *Pressure Points* video above, resulting in the complete performance at the Hammersmith Odeon. The DVD also includes a short interview with Latimer but doesn't include the video vignettes as found on the original *Pressure Points*. This is utterly infuriating but understandable as having these out of context would, I guess, be a little strange.

Coming Of Age (Released 2002)
Personnel:
Andrew Latimer: guitars, flute, vocals
Colin Bass: bass, vocals, keyboards
Dave Stewart: drums
Foss Patterson: keyboards

Originally released on VHS in 1998, this is the same set as the live album from the Billboard Live Club in Los Angeles on 13 March 1997, but with a couple of small bonuses: some rehearsal and soundcheck footage. Refer to the CD section for my critique.

Moondances. DVD. (Released 2007)
Personnel:
1976
Andrew Latimer: guitar, vocals
Peter Bardens: keyboards, vocals
Doug Ferguson: bass, vocals
Andy Ward: drums, percussion

1977
Andrew Latimer: guitar, vocals
Peter Bardens: keyboards, vocals
Richard Sinclair: bass, vocals
Andy Ward: drums, percussion
Mel Collins: Saxophone

Bonus Tracks
As for 1976

Consisting of two gigs and two bonus tracks, the sets are 50-odd minutes long. *Moondances* is a souvenir of both the *Moonmadness* and *Rain Dances* tours – hence the portmanteau title of the DVD. The first half is from the Hammersmith Odeon on 14 April 1976 and gave rise to the versions of 'White Rider' and 'Another Night' on the *A Live Record* 2002 expanded remaster, as well as the 33 rpm B-side version of 'Lunar Sea'. The second half, recorded at The Hippodrome, London on the afternoon of 22 September 1977, was a special cut-down set subsequently broadcast as one of the BBC's *Sight And Sound In Concert* series.

Sinclair's macrame guitar strap is a thing of beauty, Andy Ward's shorts, shoes and not much else, less so, but it's Latimer's pudding basin haircut and dungarees, paired with a double-neck Gibson SG, that are in clear violation of at least six of the Laws of Fashion: the 70s, eh?

Closing off the DVD, this is the sole (official) place to find the audio-only 'Autumn' and 'Riverman', leftovers from the *Moonmadness* sessions.

The Opening Farewell. DVD. (Released 2003)

Personnel:
Andrew Latimer: guitars, recorder, vocals
Colin Bass: bass, vocals
Denis Clement: drums, percussion, recorder
Tom Brislin: keyboards, backing vocals

A recording of the first show from the 2003 'Farewell Tour' recorded on 26 June 2003 at The Catalyst in Santa Cruz, California – literally down the road from Latimer and Hoover's house in Pescadero. Latimer, Bass and Clement were joined by sometime Yes, and more recently Kansas man, Tom Brislin, on keys. As mentioned, Brislin covered for Guy LeBlanc on the US leg of the tour, with Ton Scherpenzeel on point for the European leg.

As this was the tour promoting *A Nod And A Wink*, it's utterly bizarre that only one track from the album – 'For Today' – is included on the DVD: they played 'Fox Hill' that night too, but it wouldn't be until the release of *Footage II in* 2005 that we'd get to see it. That omission aside, the opening performance of 'Lady Fantasy' is sublime and the rest of the songs represent a good cross-section of Camel's back catalogue over around two hours, with the band's first song ever, 'Slow Yourself Down', 'Echoes' and 'Lunar Sea' being particular highlights.

Footage I (Released 2004) **and II** (Released 2005)

These two separately released DVDs contain a smorgasbord of visual goodies from 1973 to 2003. The simplest way to explain the contents is to list them, so here goes:

Footage I

'Never Let Go' (Guildford Civic Hall) 1973
'The Snow Goose', 'Friendship', 'Rhayader Goes To Town' (*Old Grey Whistle Test*) 1975
'First Light', 'Metrognome', 'Unevensong', 'Lunar Sea', 'Rain Dances' (BBC *Sight and Sound in Concert*) 1977
'City Life' (*Old Grey Whistle Test*) 1981
'Captured' (Hammersmith Odeon, London) 1984

'Hopeless Anger', 'Whispers in the Rain' (Town & Country Club, London) 1992
'Preparation', 'Dunkirk' (Billboard Live) 1997
'Left Luggage' (Little Barn Studios) 2003

'City Life' is the notorious mimed recording for the *Old Grey Whistle Test*, with a bereted Ward taking the piss in no small measure. The 1992 and 1997 recordings are unique to the DVD, as is the full bonus version of 'Left Luggage' from the Latimer, Ward and Ferguson reunion. The rest of the contents can be found elsewhere in the Camel DVD catalogue.

Footage II
'Arubaluba' (Guildford Civic Hall) 1973
'White Rider', 'Another Night' (Hammersmith Odeon) 1976
'Rhayader', 'Rhayader Goes To Town', 'Skylines', 'Highways of the Sun', 'Never Let Go' (BBC *Sight and Sound in Concert*) 1977
'Lies' (*Old Grey Whistle Test*) 1981
'Drafted' (Hammersmith Odeon, London) 1984
'Slow Yourself Down', 'Eyes of Ireland' (The Troubadour, Los Angeles) 2000
'Fox Hill' (The Catalyst, Santa Cruz) 2003

Footage II contains the missing 'Fox Hill' from Santa Cruz in 2003, plus previously thought lost footage of the original line up performing at the Hammersmith Odeon in 1976. 'Lies' from *Whistle Test* is another mimed performance, but the band behave themselves a little better than for 'City Life'.

I'm the first person to say that musicians deserve to be paid for their creativity, but in the case of *Footage I* and *II*, it would have been better to remove the redundancy and release a single DVD.

In From The Cold. DVD. (Released 2013)
Personnel:
Andrew Latimer: guitar, vocals, flute, recorder
Colin Bass: bass, vocals
Denis Clement: drums, percussion, recorder
Guy LeBlanc: keyboards
Jason Hart: keyboards

An emotional night, captured for posterity. When Susan Hoover announced back in 2007 that Latimer was critically ill, I think that many, if not most, fans felt this would be the end of live performances. So, when the tour was announced, at first, you had to pinch yourself to make sure that this wasn't some sort of impish dream. But Latimer had recovered, and Camel were back.

Recorded live at The Barbican, London on 28 October 2013, the set comprises the whole of *Snow Goose* as well as a fine cross-section of favourites. Helping out with the orchestrations, Renaissance man Jason Hart joined on keys to support Guy LeBlanc. There is no CD version of the concert, so this is the only way to hear the marvellous resurrection of the band.

Ichigo Ichie – Camel Live In Japan. DVD. (Released 2016)
Personnel:
Andrew Latimer: guitar, vocals, flute, recorder
Colin Bass: bass, vocals
Denis Clement: drums, percussion, recorder
Pete Jones: keyboards, vocals, pennywhistle

Camel did a mini, four-date tour of Japan in 2016, and *Ichigo Ichie* (translated as 'Treasure every encounter as it will never recur') was recorded on the second of two nights at the EX Theatre in Tokyo on 21 May 2016. It's a landmark in the recent history of the band as it's the first recorded appearance of Pete Jones on keyboards. So accomplished is his playing that you'd never know that it was only a few weeks before the gig that he first rehearsed with Camel.

Setlist-wise, it's a little unadventurous – certainly when compared to the *Opening Farewell* set and, to a lesser extent, *In From The Cold*. Production quality, though, is exceptional. Again, as for *In From The Cold*, there is no CD version available.

Camel: Live At The Royal Albert Hall, 2018 (DVD / BluRay) (Released 2020)
Personnel:
Andrew Latimer: guitar, vocals, flute, recorder
Colin Bass: bass, vocals
Denis Clement: drums, percussion, recorder
Pete Jones: keyboards, vocals, penny whistle

The magic in all its glory, including Jones on sax during 'Rajaz'. It's hard for me not to go all misty-eyed about this video. The performance was magnificent in every conceivable way: the setlist, the performances, the atmosphere, the emotions and, naturally, the setting itself. Camel came home that night, and what a night it was.

Due to a logistical screw-up – the original video company hired to shoot the concert pulled out a few days ahead – for a time, the band were resigned to not having the gig filmed. As a result, some of the seats that were reserved for cameras were made available and sold (remember, the concert was sold out, so additional tix were like gold dust). At the last minute, another company stepped in to film the concert, but due to those now-sold seats, they were unable to cover all the angles specified in the original production schedule. Nevertheless, once you're immersed in the music, I doubt you'll notice.

We, of course, kick off with the playing of *Moonmadness* in full. On the basis of this performance, the LP hasn't dated a second since its release in 1976: in fact, it sounds fresher than ever, the running order and song construction peerless to this day. What follows is a selection of old live favourites – I won't dwell on the setlist, save for again mentioning 'Rajaz' and 'Mother Road', showcases for Pete Jones' outstanding talent.

Suffice to say, as a Camel fan, you have to own this.

Above: Camel in full swing during 'Lunar Sea' at the Royal Albert Hall in October 2018. (*Geir Stavseng*)

Below: 'Thank you, London': the band looking happy but understandably shell-shocked after another legendary sold-out performance and the end of the 'story so far'. (*Geir Stavseng*)

139

Further Listening, Watching and Reading
Listening
Music Directly Related To Camel Members:
Philip Goodhand-Tait
I Think I'll Write a Song
(LP rip freely available on the web, the physical album is somewhat harder to come by, but a vinyl copy pops up now and again on-line)

Peter Bardens
The Answer (1970)
Peter Bardens (*Write My Name In The Dust* in the U.S.) (1971)
Vintage 69 (1976)
Heart To Heart (1979)
Seen One Earth (1987)
Speed Of Light (1988)
Water Colors (1991)
Further Than You Know (1993)
Big Sky (1994)
The Art Of Levitation (2002)
Write My Name In The Dust: The Anthology 1963–2002 (2005)

Andy Ward
Solo
Sticking Around (2003)

With The Bevis Frond
Superseeder (1995)

With Caravan of Dreams
Richard Sinclair's Caravan Of Dreams (1992)

With Anton Barbeau
King Of Missouri (2002)

Colin Bass
Solo
As Far as I Can See EP (1998)
Gently Kindly (2002)
Planetarium (With Józef Skrzek) (2005)
In the Meantime – Remastered + 5 bonus tracks (2006)
An Outcast of the Islands – Reissue (2012)
At Wild End (2015)
As Sabah Habas Mustapha
Jalan Kopo (1998)

So La Li (1999)
Denpasar Moon 2004 – remastered + bonus (2004)

With 3 Mustaphas 3
Orchestra BAM de Grand Mustapha International and (Jolly) Party – Local Music (1986)
Shopping (1987)
Soup of the Century (1990)
Friends, Fiends & Fronds (1991)
Play Musty for Me (2001)

Jan Schelhaas
Dark Ships (2008)
Living On A Little Blue Dot (2017)
Ghosts Of Eden (2018)

Peter Jones / Tiger Moth Tales
Cocoon (2014)
Story Tellers – Part 1 (2015)
Depths of Winter (2017)
Story Tellers – Part 2 (2018)
Still Alive (2020)
The Whispering Of The World (2020)

Kayak (Ton Scherpenzeel)
Seventeen (2018)

Nathan Mahl (Guy LeBlanc)
Parallel Eccentricities (1983)
The Clever Use of Shadows (1998)

Watching
Camel Productions YouTube Channel – a source of some lovely 'behind the scenes' gems.
Peter Bardens (Mirage and Solo) – multiple videos on YouTube

Reading
Paul Gallico – *The Snow Goose* (ISBN-10: 9780140299526)
John Steinbeck – *The Grapes of Wrath* (ISBN-10: 9780141185064)
Turtle Bunbury – *The Irish Diaspora: Tales of Emigration, Exile and Imperialism* (ISBN-10: 0500022526)
Chris Morton – Andy Ward, Musical Tales (https://chrismortonphotostories.co.uk/andy-ward-musical-tales)

And, of course, all the excellent sleeve notes contained in the remastered CDs.

The 'Ultimate' Playlists

Last but not least, here are two playlists: the first is the author's 'Best Of' – a Camel mix-tape of the old school, if you will. Deliberately not chronological, it averages two tracks from the fourteen studio albums.

'Sasquatch'
'Rajaz'
'Supertwister'
'Unevensong'
'Wait'
'Lady Fantasy'
'Rhayader' / 'Rhayader Goes To Town'
'The Snow Goose'
'Song Within A Song'
'Metrognome'
'Echoes'
'Down On The Farm'
'The Sleeper'
'Pressure Points'
'Send Home The Slates'
'A Nod And A Wink'
'Mother Road'
'End of the Line'
'Hopeless Anger'
'Hymn To Her'
'City Life'
'Captured'
'Dunkirk'
'Watching The Bobbins'
'Three Wishes'
'Stationary Traveller'
'Ice'
'Lunar Sea'
'Fox Hill'
'Never Let Go'

The second is a 62-minute chronological collection of Camel's 'fusion' output, starting with a live version of 'Homage To The Gods Of Light': I would dearly love Andy and Susan to release this as a CD as it would showcase an often overlooked but critical aspect of the band's output. I'll even suggest a name for the collection, which they would be welcome to purloin: ' *'Nice' – Camel Play Jazz-Rock Fusion*

'Homage To The Gods Of Light'
'Supertwister'

'Liggin' at Louis''
'Chord Change'
'Lunar Sea'
'One Of These Days I'll Get An Early Night'
'Skylines'
'The Sleeper'

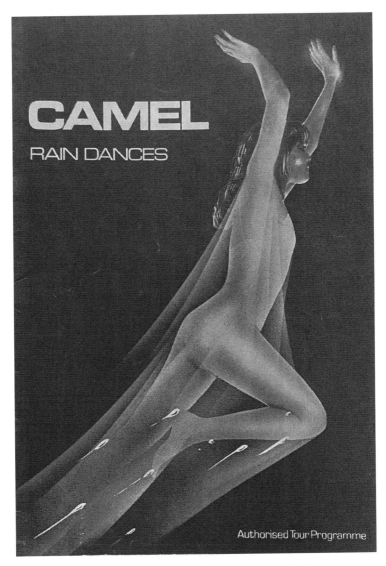

Above: *Rain Dances* UK tour programme from 1977. (*Private collection of Shane Carlson*)

Would you like to write for Sonicbond Publishing?

At Sonicbond Publishing we are always on the look-out for authors, particularly for our two main series:

On Track. Mixing fact with in depth analysis, the On Track series examines the work of a particular musical artist or group. All genres are considered from easy listening and jazz to 60s soul to 90s pop, via rock and metal.

On Screen. This series looks at the world of film and television. Subjects considered include directors, actors and writers, as well as entire television and film series. As with the On Track series, we balance fact with analysis.

While professional writing experience would, of course, be an advantage the most important qualification is to have real enthusiasm and knowledge of your subject. First-time authors are welcomed, but the ability to write well in English is essential.

Sonicbond Publishing has distribution throughout Europe and North America, and all books are also published in E-book form. Authors will be paid a royalty based on sales of their book.

Further details are available from www.sonicbondpublishing.co.uk. To contact us, complete the contact form there or email info@sonicbondpublishing.co.uk